A WHO HQ GRAPHIC NOVEL

Who Was Her Own Work of Art?

FRIDA K

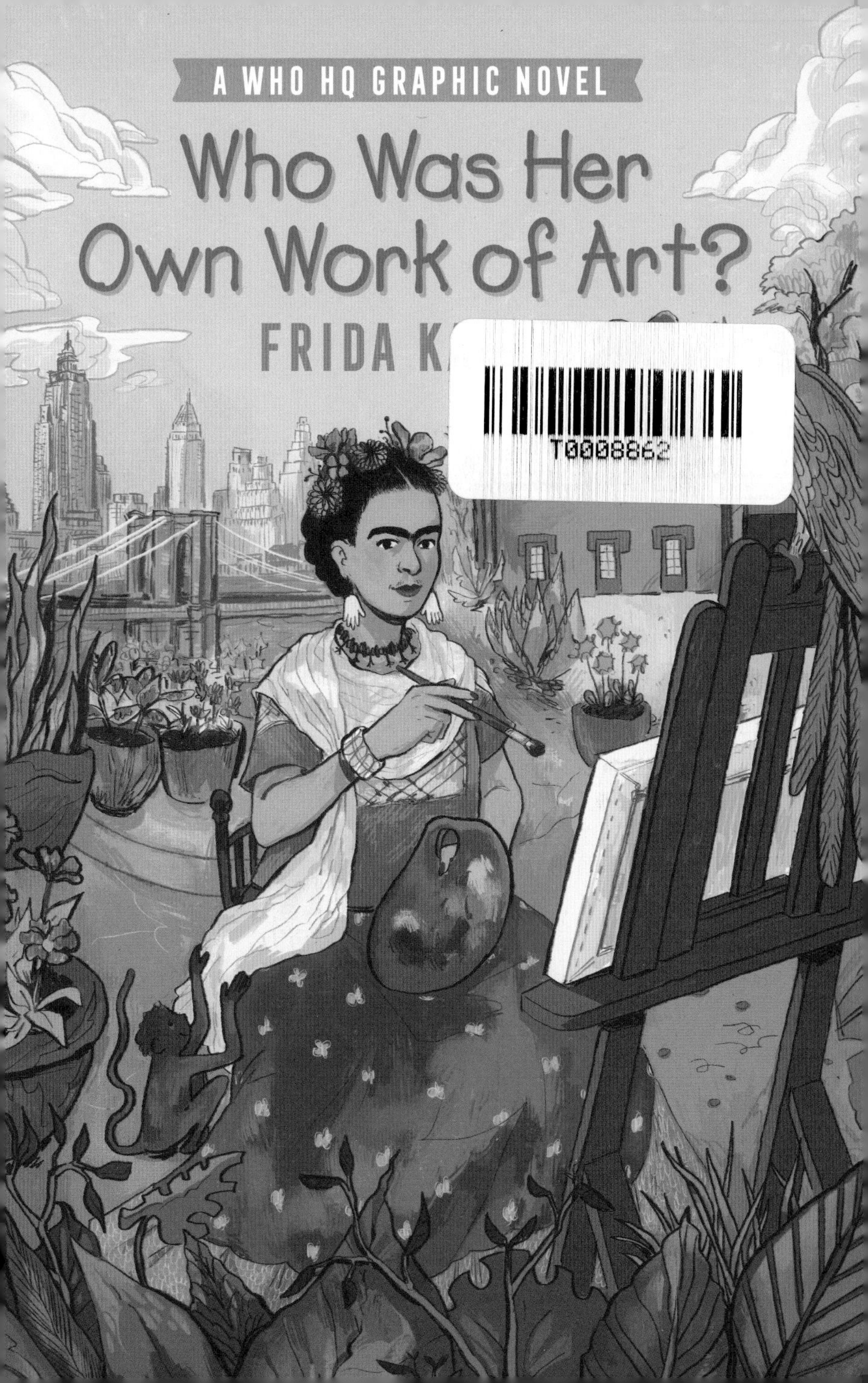

For Lanny–You always encouraged me to make art
and to be proud of my heritage–TB

To all my fellow weird girls. Our lives and stories are worth
celebrating. A mi mamá también, como siempre–AF

PENGUIN WORKSHOP
An imprint of Penguin Random House LLC, New York

First published in the United States of America by Penguin Workshop,
an imprint of Penguin Random House LLC, New York, 2024

Visit us online at penguinrandomhouse.com.

Library of Congress Cataloging-in-Publication Data is available.

Manufactured in China

ISBN 9780593384657 (pbk)   10 9 8 7 6 5 4 3 2 1 HH
ISBN 9780593384664 (hc)   10 9 8 7 6 5 4 3 2 1 HH

Lettering by Comicraft
Design by Mary Claire Cruz

This is a work of nonfiction. All of the events that unfold in the narrative
are rooted in historical fact. Some dialogue and characters have been fictionalized
in order to illustrate or teach a historical point.

The publisher does not have any control over and does not assume
any responsibility for author or third-party websites or their content.

For more information about your favorite historical figures, places, and events,
please visit whohq.com.

A WHO HQ GRAPHIC NOVEL

Who Was Her Own Work of Art?

FRIDA KAHLO

by Terry Blas
illustrated by Ashanti Fortson

Penguin Workshop

Introduction

On September 17, 1925, when the young Mexican student Frida Kahlo (born Magdalena Carmen Frida Kahlo y Calderón) was just eighteen years old, she got into a terrible bus accident. It left her with many physical ailments and injuries that affected her greatly. She was bedridden and put in a plaster body cast. Not being able to move around, her parents had a special easel made for her and installed a mirror above her bed so that she could return to a hobby she had loved as a little child: drawing and painting. This ignited a passion in Frida, who from then on always wanted to paint her reality—even if her reality was sometimes not a happy one.

Making art was the way she felt she could express herself, but in the summer of 1938, Frida started to feel restless. She was thirty-one years old and consistently felt like she was in the shadow of her husband, prominent Mexican painter Diego Rivera, who was known for his vast, vibrantly colored murals that portrayed life in the heart of Mexico City.

Frida was a painter, too, but not many people knew this.

In the early years of her marriage to Diego, the couple traveled a lot to show Diego's art to the world. From New York City to Detroit to Paris, the couple

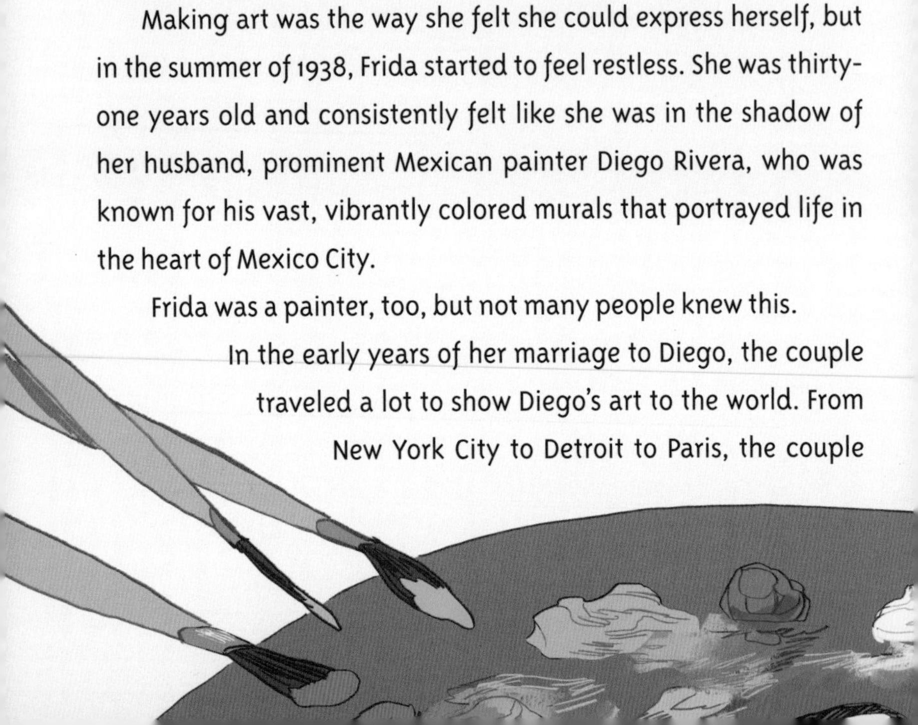

was exposed to the world but also to various international art movements of the time, such as surrealism.

But Frida wanted more independence, financially and emotionally. She was encouraged by many to show her art in an attempt to help support herself. Frida's family, friends, and even Diego wanted the world to know more about Frida and her work. Her identity itself was a matter of public fascination: Her father was German and her mother was a mestiza, or mixed-race, Mexican woman, so she grew up in a very multicultural household. Not to mention, Frida also became a passionate member of the Mexican Communist Party at a young age and wanted to show her Mexican heritage and pride to the world.

Slowly, she began to show her work to the public. In September of 1937, with Diego's encouragement, some of Frida's paintings were hung in a group exhibition at the Galería de Arte at the Universidad Nacional Autónoma de México in Mexico City. The following year, French surrealist author André Breton visited her studio to see her work, and this led to her gaining more attention from her artistic peers.

Frida felt the urge to be regarded as her own person and not just as her husband's wife. She longed to know if she could be seen as someone who was not only acknowledged by the art world but who lit it on fire.

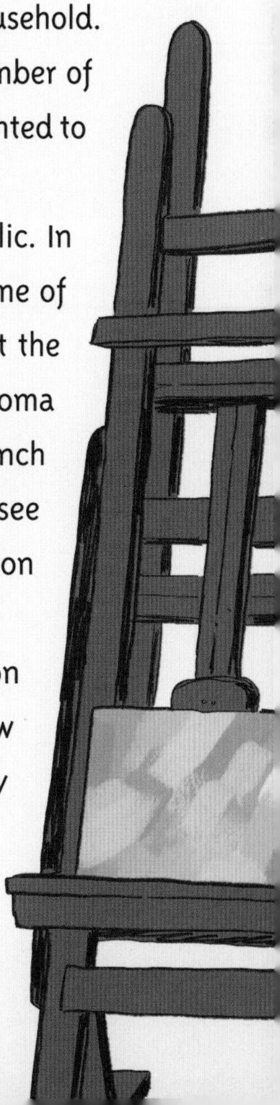

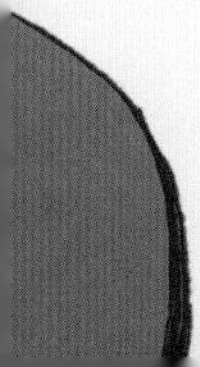

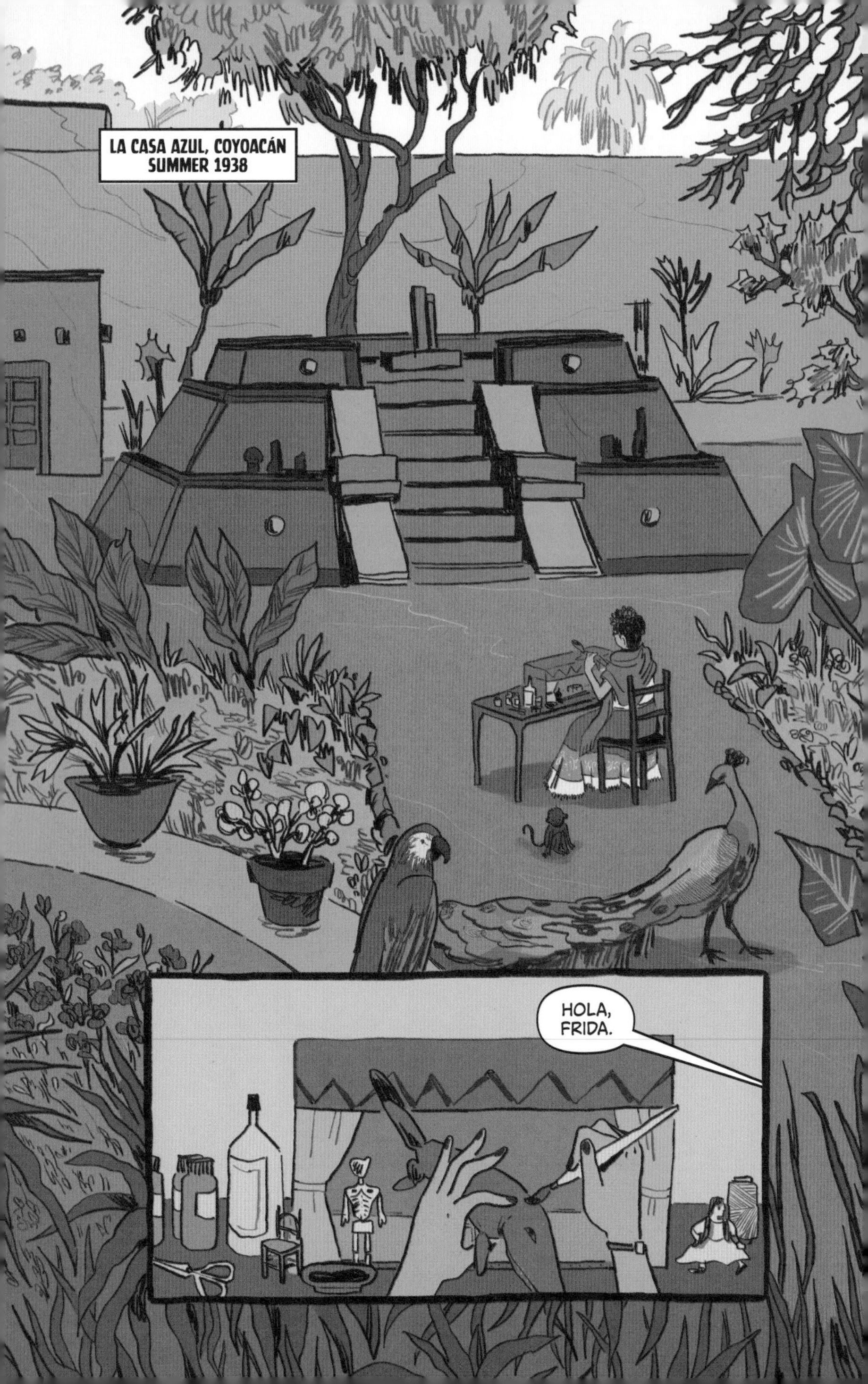
LA CASA AZUL, COYOACÁN
SUMMER 1938
HOLA, FRIDA.

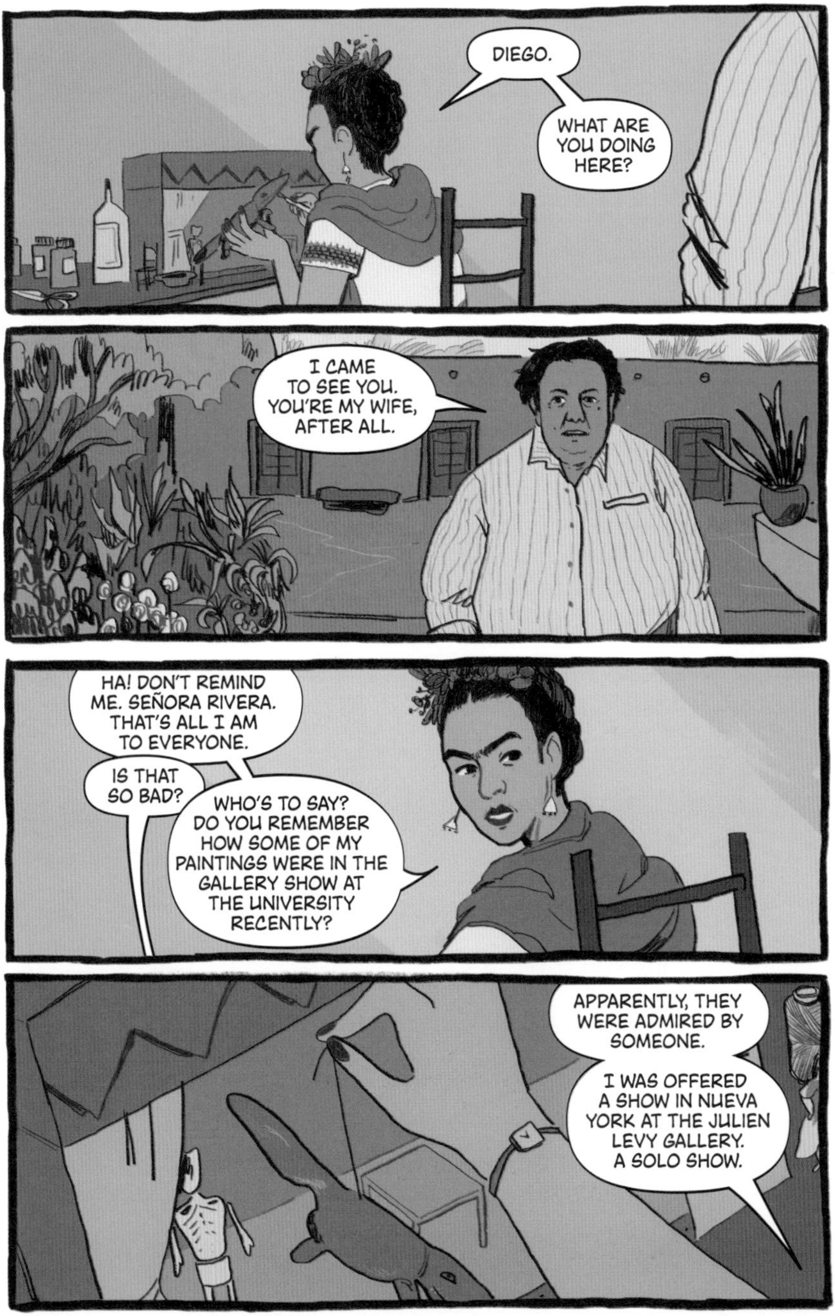
DIEGO.
WHAT ARE YOU DOING HERE?
I CAME TO SEE YOU. YOU'RE MY WIFE, AFTER ALL.
HA! DON'T REMIND ME. SEÑORA RIVERA. THAT'S ALL I AM TO EVERYONE.
IS THAT SO BAD?
WHO'S TO SAY? DO YOU REMEMBER HOW SOME OF MY PAINTINGS WERE IN THE GALLERY SHOW AT THE UNIVERSITY RECENTLY?
APPARENTLY, THEY WERE ADMIRED BY SOMEONE.
I WAS OFFERED A SHOW IN NUEVA YORK AT THE JULIEN LEVY GALLERY. A SOLO SHOW.

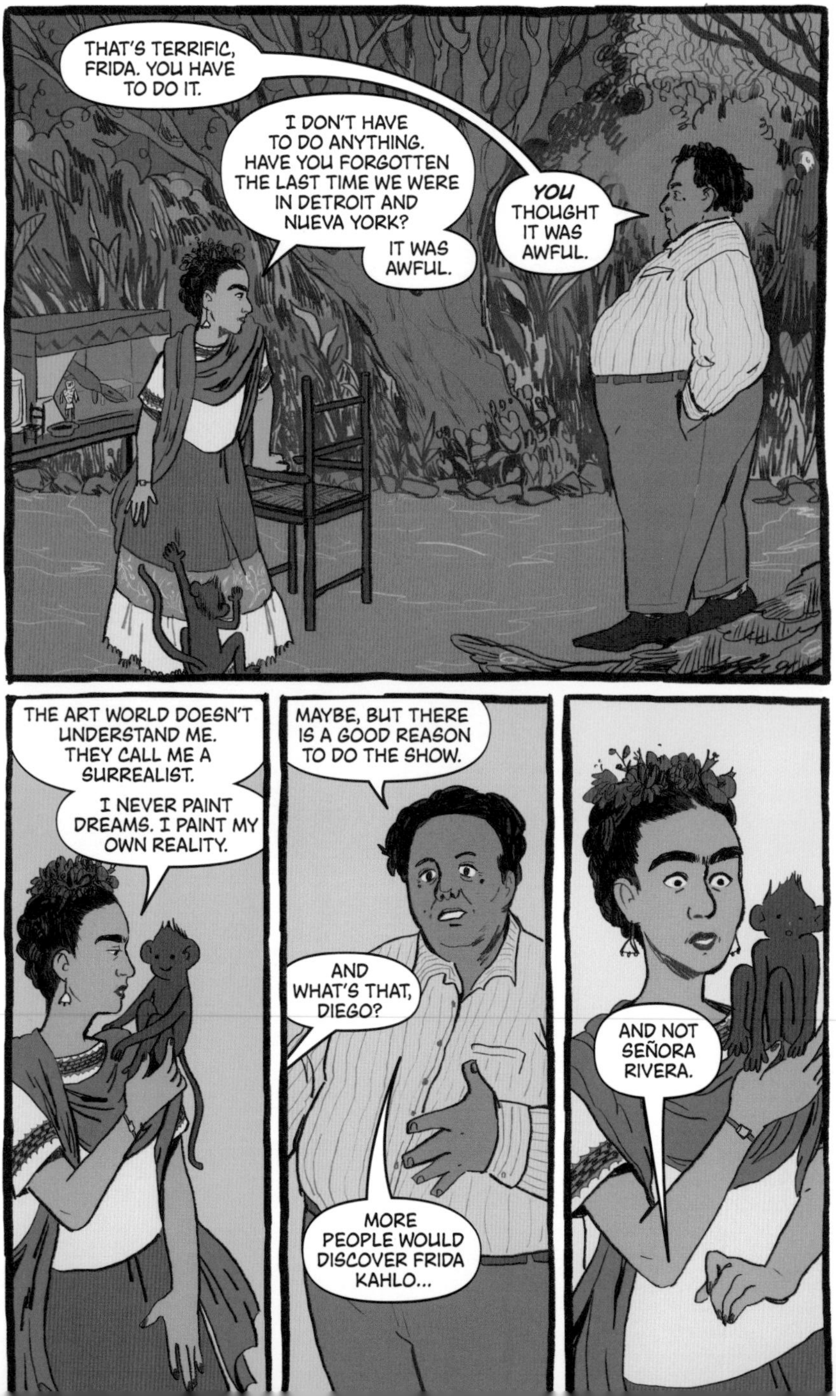
THAT'S TERRIFIC, FRIDA. YOU HAVE TO DO IT.
I DON'T HAVE TO DO ANYTHING. HAVE YOU FORGOTTEN THE LAST TIME WE WERE IN DETROIT AND NUEVA YORK?
IT WAS AWFUL.
YOU THOUGHT IT WAS AWFUL.
THE ART WORLD DOESN'T UNDERSTAND ME. THEY CALL ME A SURREALIST.
I NEVER PAINT DREAMS. I PAINT MY OWN REALITY.
MAYBE, BUT THERE IS A GOOD REASON TO DO THE SHOW.
AND WHAT'S THAT, DIEGO?
MORE PEOPLE WOULD DISCOVER FRIDA KAHLO...
AND NOT SEÑORA RIVERA.

Diego Rivera

Diego Rivera was born on December 8, 1886, in Guanajuato, Mexico, to María del Pilar Barrientos and Diego Rivera Acosta.

Diego loved painting from an early age. When he was ten years old, he began studying art at the Academy of San Carlos in Mexico City, and in 1907, when he was twenty-one, he studied an art movement called Cubism in Europe.

Diego wanted to depict the lives of everyday Mexican people and make art accessible to everyone. In 1922, he joined the Revolutionary Union of Technical Workers, Painters, and Sculptors, and he became an advocate of the Mexican Communist Party. From then on, Diego only painted murals, usually on public buildings, using fresco—a technique of painting large-scale art directly onto walls. That same year, Diego painted his first widely-known mural, *Creation*, for the National Preparatory School in Mexico City.

This helped establish the mural movement in Mexico and abroad, and Diego was hired to paint many murals that explored everyday contemporary social and political issues, such as the *History of Mexico* frescoes in Mexico's National Palace and *Man at the Crossroads* in New York City's Rockefeller Center.

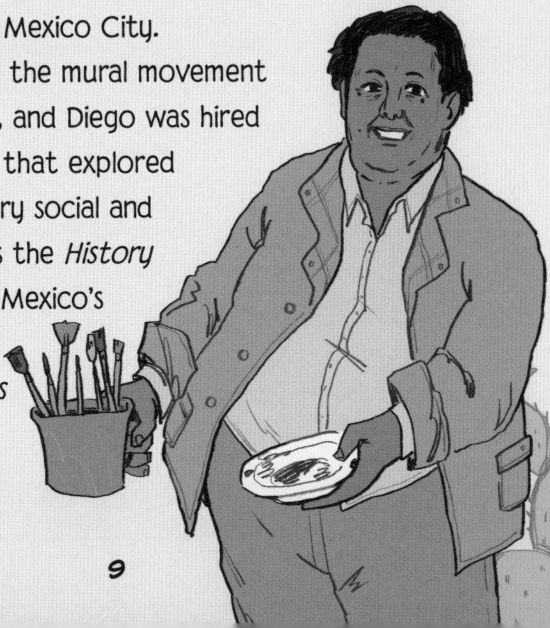

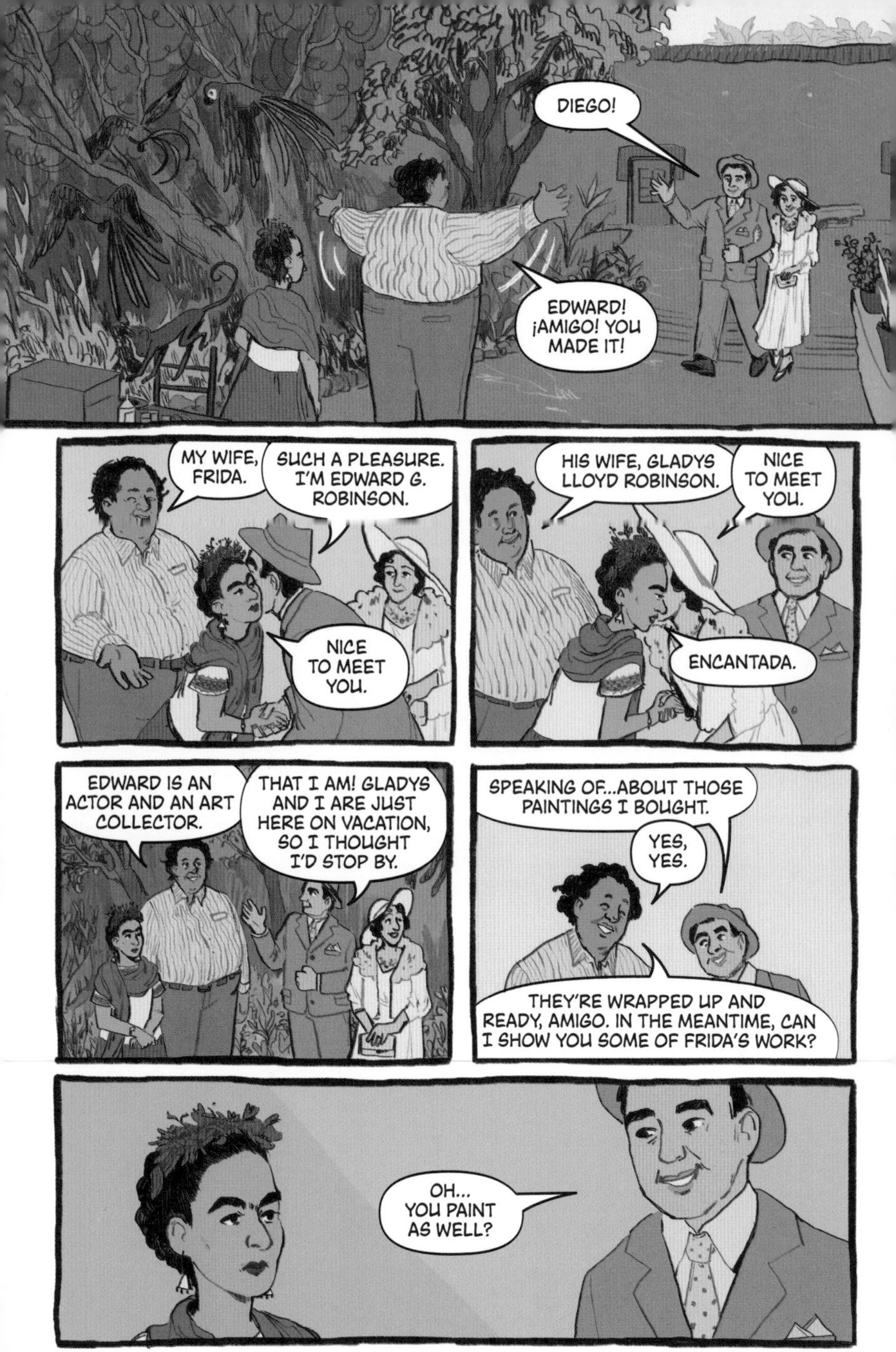
DIEGO!
EDWARD! ¡AMIGO! YOU MADE IT!
MY WIFE, FRIDA.
SUCH A PLEASURE. I'M EDWARD G. ROBINSON.
NICE TO MEET YOU.
HIS WIFE, GLADYS LLOYD ROBINSON.
NICE TO MEET YOU.
ENCANTADA.
EDWARD IS AN ACTOR AND AN ART COLLECTOR.
THAT I AM! GLADYS AND I ARE JUST HERE ON VACATION, SO I THOUGHT I'D STOP BY.
SPEAKING OF...ABOUT THOSE PAINTINGS I BOUGHT.
YES, YES.
THEY'RE WRAPPED UP AND READY, AMIGO. IN THE MEANTIME, CAN I SHOW YOU SOME OF FRIDA'S WORK?
OH... YOU PAINT AS WELL?

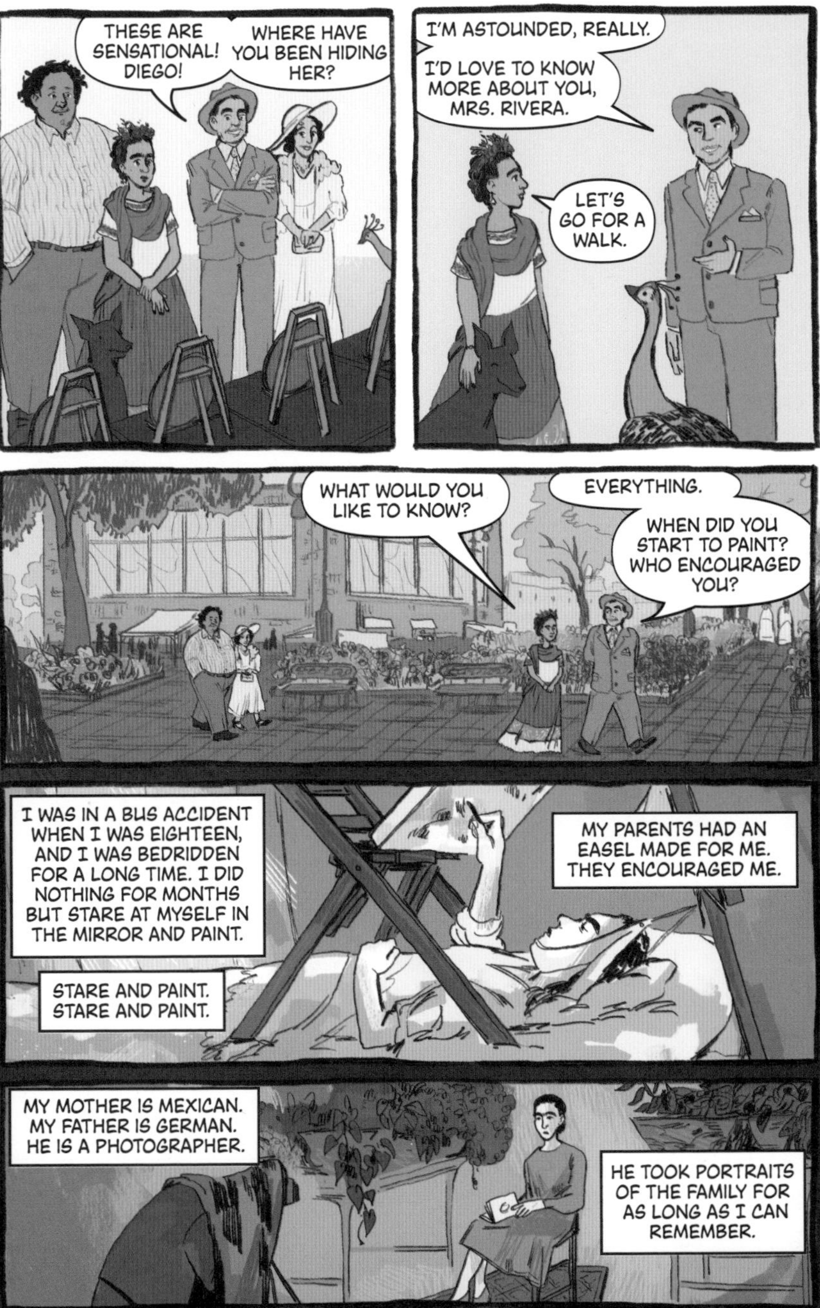
THESE ARE SENSATIONAL! DIEGO!
WHERE HAVE YOU BEEN HIDING HER?
I'M ASTOUNDED, REALLY.
I'D LOVE TO KNOW MORE ABOUT YOU, MRS. RIVERA.
LET'S GO FOR A WALK.
WHAT WOULD YOU LIKE TO KNOW?
EVERYTHING.
WHEN DID YOU START TO PAINT? WHO ENCOURAGED YOU?
I WAS IN A BUS ACCIDENT WHEN I WAS EIGHTEEN, AND I WAS BEDRIDDEN FOR A LONG TIME. I DID NOTHING FOR MONTHS BUT STARE AT MYSELF IN THE MIRROR AND PAINT.
STARE AND PAINT. STARE AND PAINT.
MY PARENTS HAD AN EASEL MADE FOR ME. THEY ENCOURAGED ME.
MY MOTHER IS MEXICAN. MY FATHER IS GERMAN. HE IS A PHOTOGRAPHER.
HE TOOK PORTRAITS OF THE FAMILY FOR AS LONG AS I CAN REMEMBER.

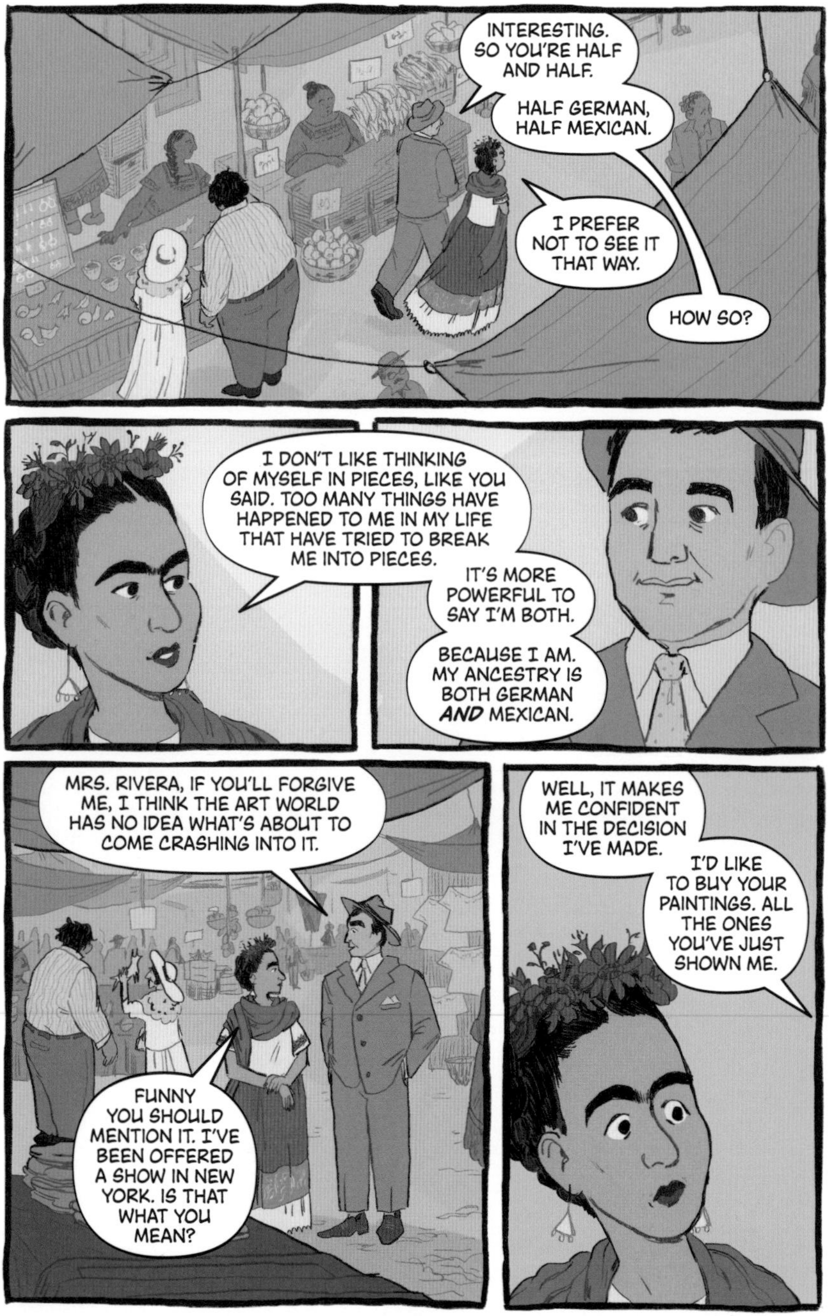
INTERESTING. SO YOU'RE HALF AND HALF.
HALF GERMAN, HALF MEXICAN.
I PREFER NOT TO SEE IT THAT WAY.
HOW SO?
I DON'T LIKE THINKING OF MYSELF IN PIECES, LIKE YOU SAID. TOO MANY THINGS HAVE HAPPENED TO ME IN MY LIFE THAT HAVE TRIED TO BREAK ME INTO PIECES.
IT'S MORE POWERFUL TO SAY I'M BOTH.
BECAUSE I AM. MY ANCESTRY IS BOTH GERMAN ***AND*** MEXICAN.
MRS. RIVERA, IF YOU'LL FORGIVE ME, I THINK THE ART WORLD HAS NO IDEA WHAT'S ABOUT TO COME CRASHING INTO IT.
FUNNY YOU SHOULD MENTION IT. I'VE BEEN OFFERED A SHOW IN NEW YORK. IS THAT WHAT YOU MEAN?
WELL, IT MAKES ME CONFIDENT IN THE DECISION I'VE MADE.
I'D LIKE TO BUY YOUR PAINTINGS. ALL THE ONES YOU'VE JUST SHOWN ME.

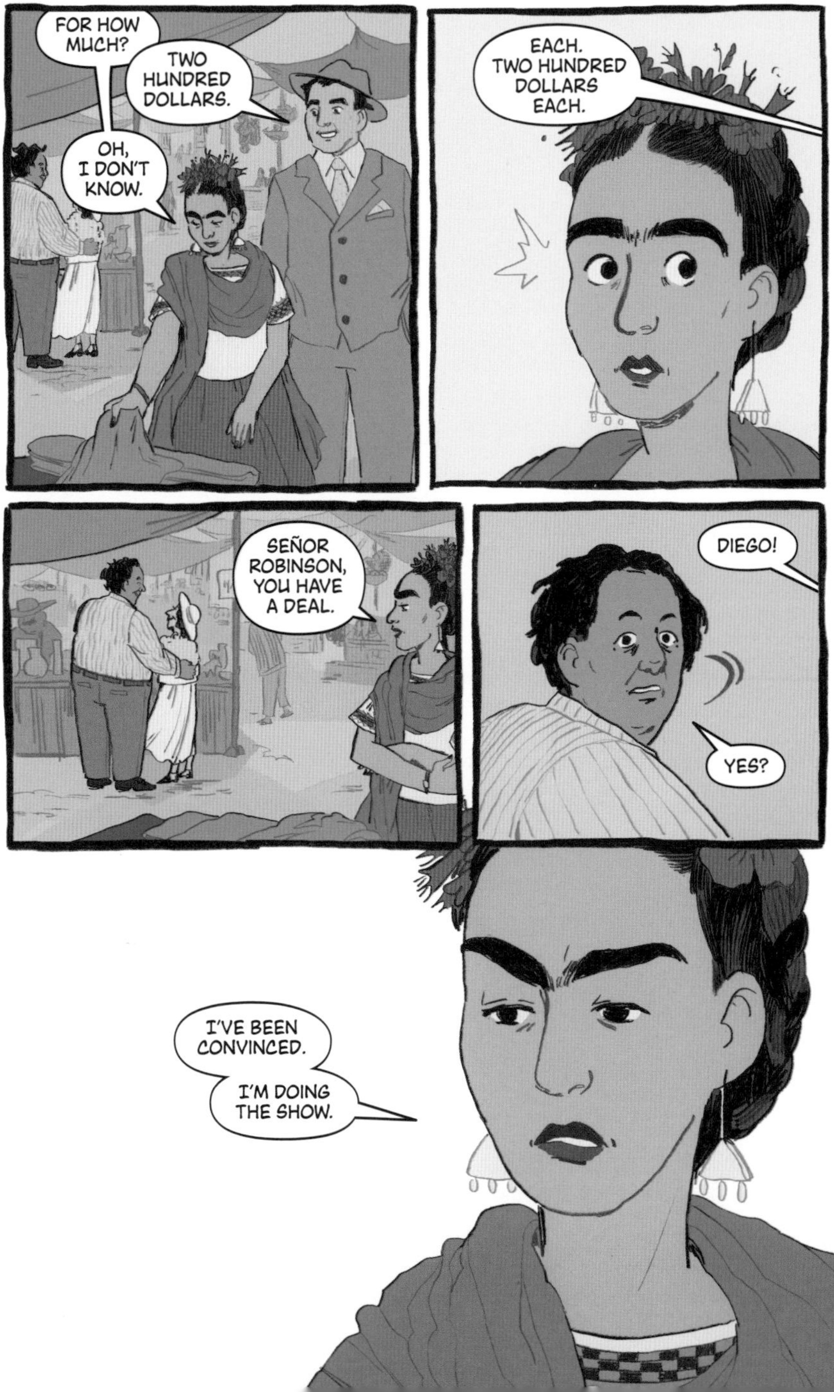
FOR HOW MUCH?
TWO HUNDRED DOLLARS.
OH, I DON'T KNOW.
EACH. TWO HUNDRED DOLLARS EACH.
SEÑOR ROBINSON, YOU HAVE A DEAL.
DIEGO!
YES?
I'VE BEEN CONVINCED.
I'M DOING THE SHOW.

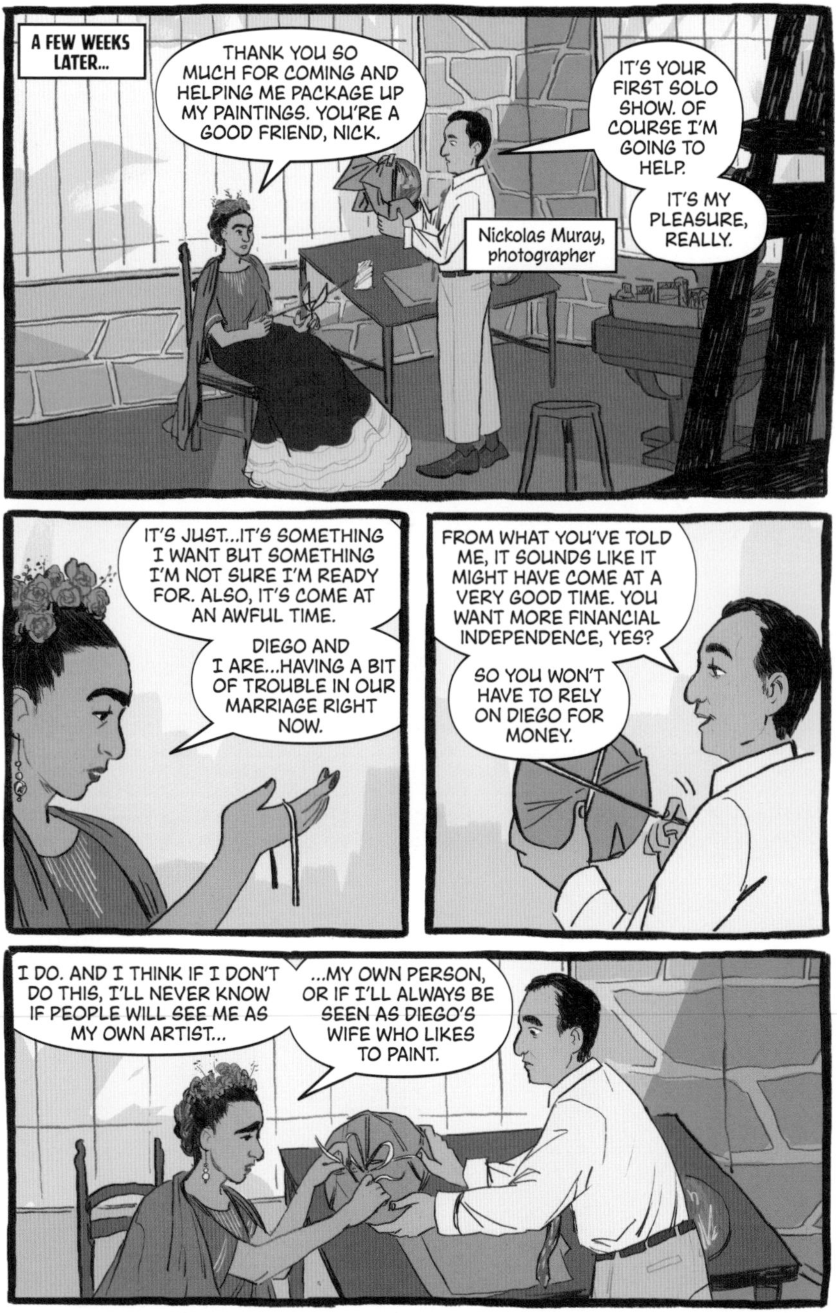
A FEW WEEKS LATER...
THANK YOU SO MUCH FOR COMING AND HELPING ME PACKAGE UP MY PAINTINGS. YOU'RE A GOOD FRIEND, NICK.
IT'S YOUR FIRST SOLO SHOW. OF COURSE I'M GOING TO HELP.
IT'S MY PLEASURE, REALLY.
Nickolas Muray, photographer
IT'S JUST...IT'S SOMETHING I WANT BUT SOMETHING I'M NOT SURE I'M READY FOR. ALSO, IT'S COME AT AN AWFUL TIME.
DIEGO AND I ARE...HAVING A BIT OF TROUBLE IN OUR MARRIAGE RIGHT NOW.
FROM WHAT YOU'VE TOLD ME, IT SOUNDS LIKE IT MIGHT HAVE COME AT A VERY GOOD TIME. YOU WANT MORE FINANCIAL INDEPENDENCE, YES?
SO YOU WON'T HAVE TO RELY ON DIEGO FOR MONEY.
I DO. AND I THINK IF I DON'T DO THIS, I'LL NEVER KNOW IF PEOPLE WILL SEE ME AS MY OWN ARTIST...
...MY OWN PERSON, OR IF I'LL ALWAYS BE SEEN AS DIEGO'S WIFE WHO LIKES TO PAINT.

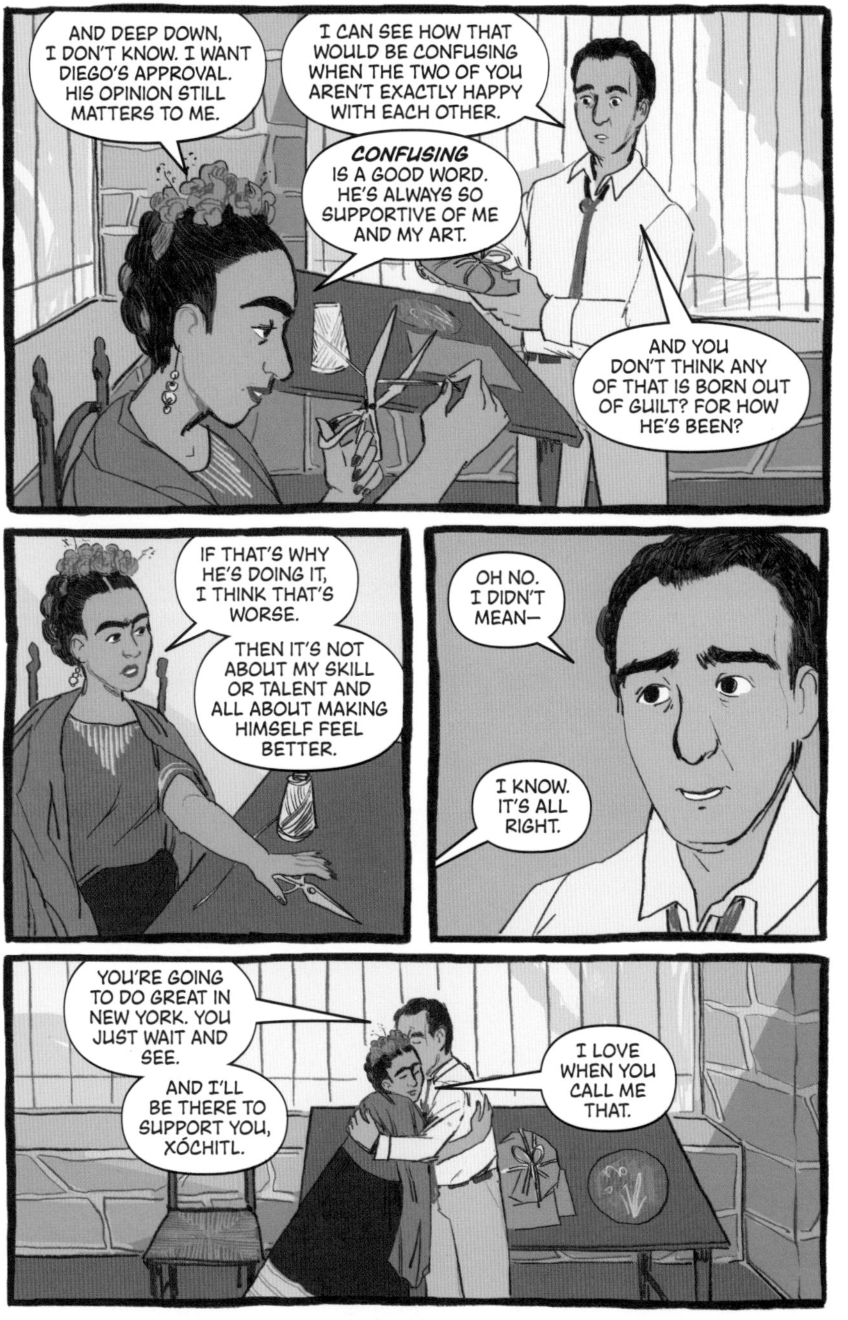
AND DEEP DOWN, I DON'T KNOW. I WANT DIEGO'S APPROVAL. HIS OPINION STILL MATTERS TO ME.
I CAN SEE HOW THAT WOULD BE CONFUSING WHEN THE TWO OF YOU AREN'T EXACTLY HAPPY WITH EACH OTHER.
CONFUSING IS A GOOD WORD. HE'S ALWAYS SO SUPPORTIVE OF ME AND MY ART.
AND YOU DON'T THINK ANY OF THAT IS BORN OUT OF GUILT? FOR HOW HE'S BEEN?
IF THAT'S WHY HE'S DOING IT, I THINK THAT'S WORSE.
THEN IT'S NOT ABOUT MY SKILL OR TALENT AND ALL ABOUT MAKING HIMSELF FEEL BETTER.
OH NO. I DIDN'T MEAN—
I KNOW. IT'S ALL RIGHT.
YOU'RE GOING TO DO GREAT IN NEW YORK. YOU JUST WAIT AND SEE.
AND I'LL BE THERE TO SUPPORT YOU, XÓCHITL.
I LOVE WHEN YOU CALL ME THAT.

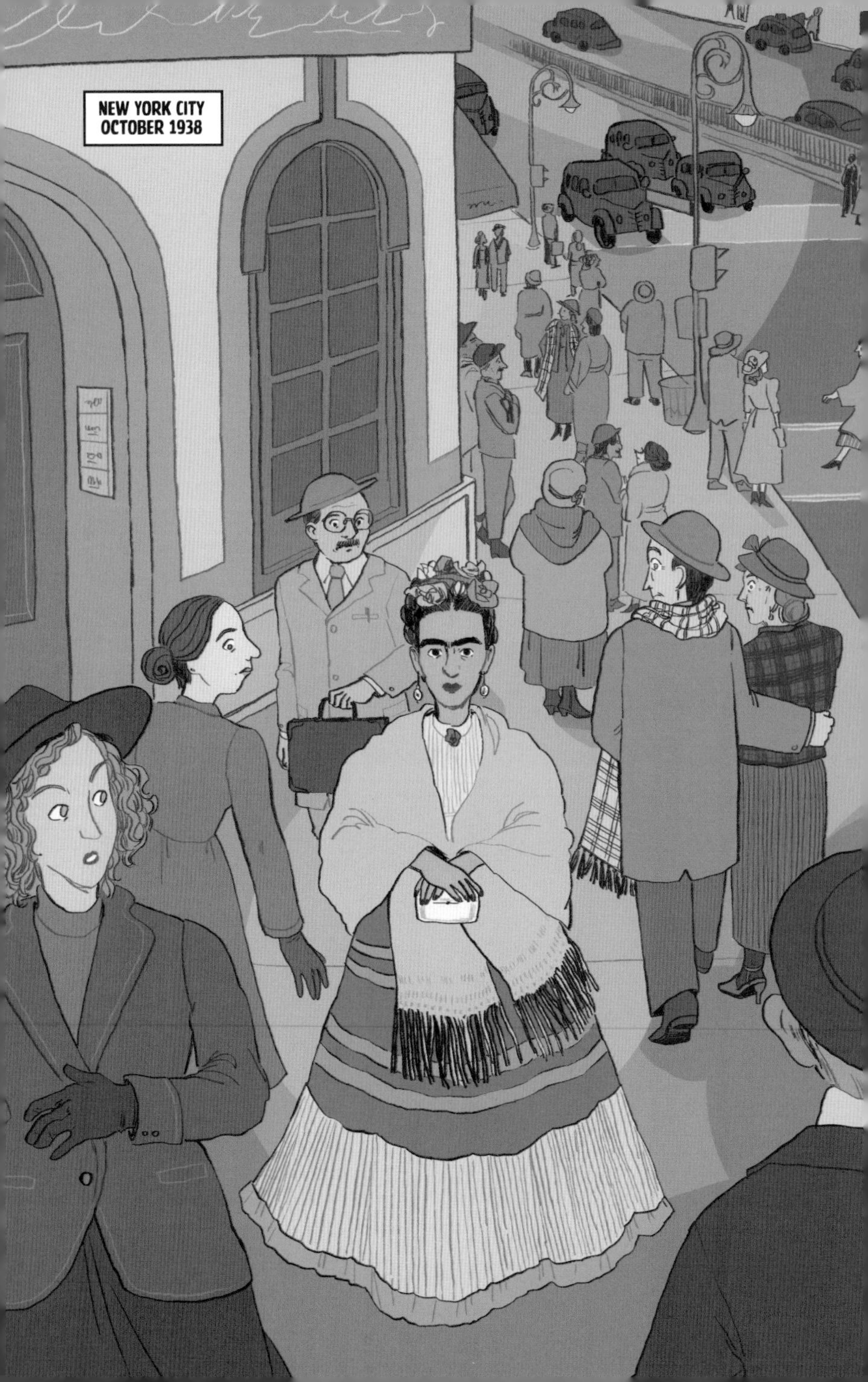
NEW YORK CITY
OCTOBER 1938

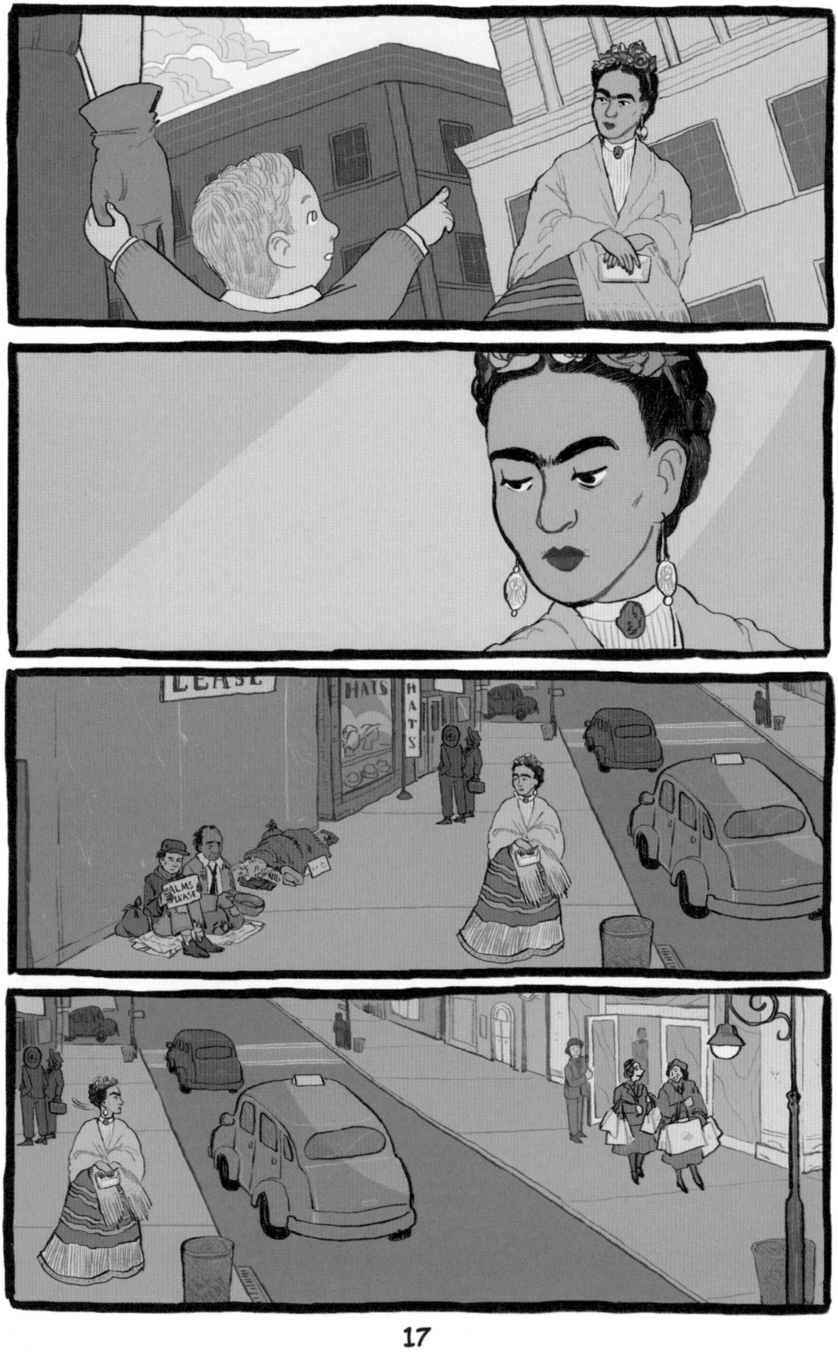
LEASE
HATS
HATS
ALMS PLEASE

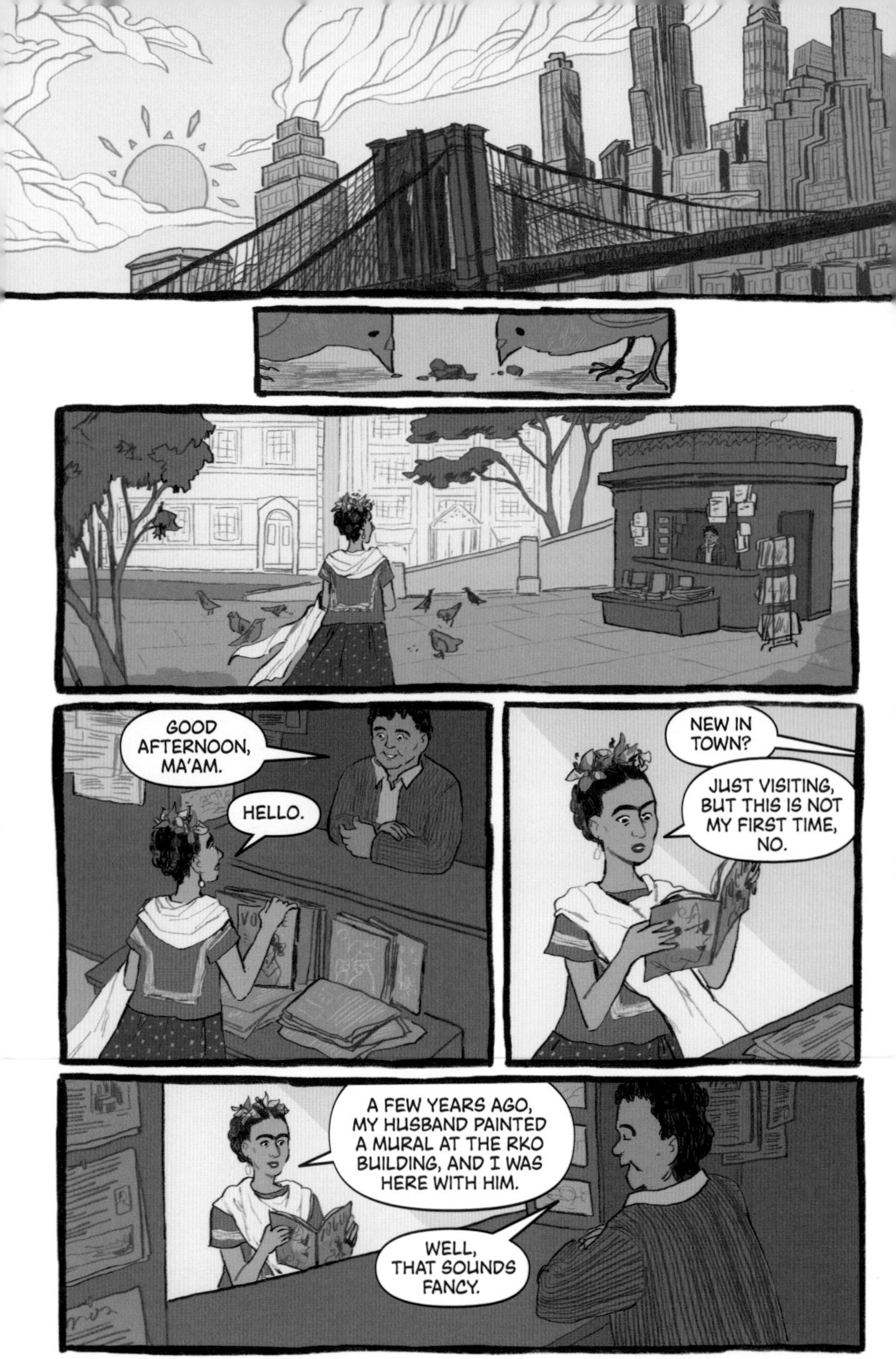
GOOD AFTERNOON, MA'AM.
HELLO.
NEW IN TOWN?
JUST VISITING, BUT THIS IS NOT MY FIRST TIME, NO.
A FEW YEARS AGO, MY HUSBAND PAINTED A MURAL AT THE RKO BUILDING, AND I WAS HERE WITH HIM.
WELL, THAT SOUNDS FANCY.

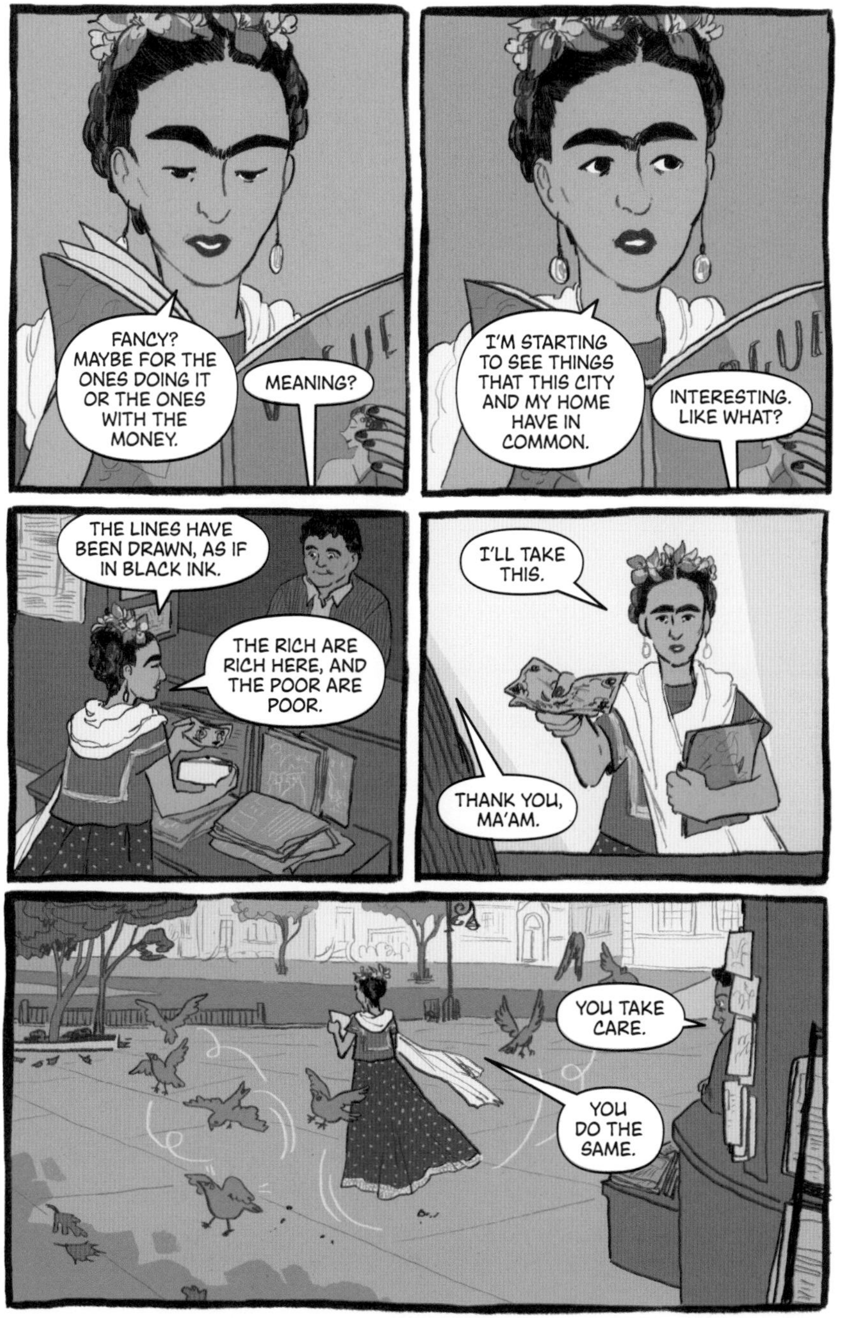
FANCY? MAYBE FOR THE ONES DOING IT OR THE ONES WITH THE MONEY.
MEANING?
I'M STARTING TO SEE THINGS THAT THIS CITY AND MY HOME HAVE IN COMMON.
INTERESTING. LIKE WHAT?
THE LINES HAVE BEEN DRAWN, AS IF IN BLACK INK.
THE RICH ARE RICH HERE, AND THE POOR ARE POOR.
I'LL TAKE THIS.
THANK YOU, MA'AM.
YOU TAKE CARE.
YOU DO THE SAME.

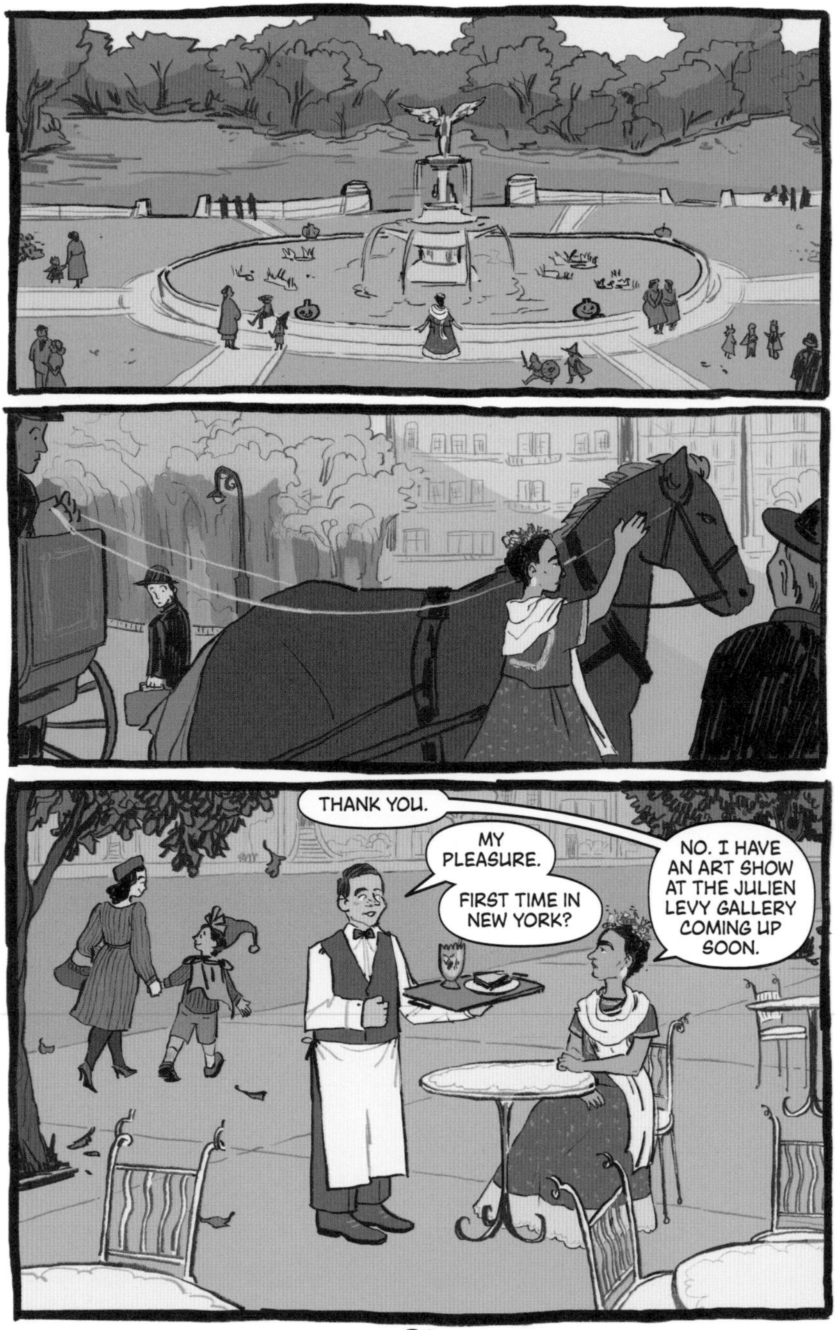
THANK YOU.
MY PLEASURE.
FIRST TIME IN NEW YORK?
NO. I HAVE AN ART SHOW AT THE JULIEN LEVY GALLERY COMING UP SOON.

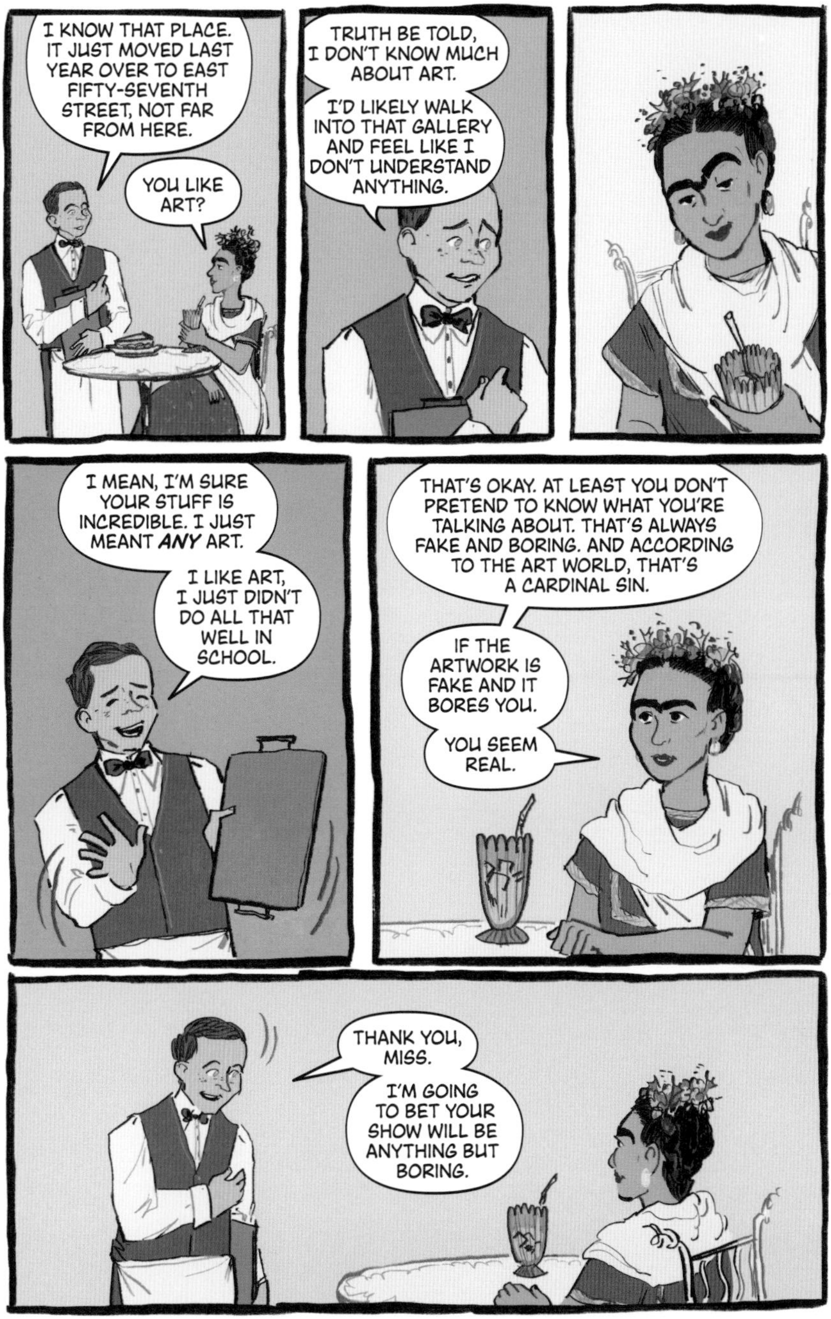
I KNOW THAT PLACE. IT JUST MOVED LAST YEAR OVER TO EAST FIFTY-SEVENTH STREET, NOT FAR FROM HERE.
YOU LIKE ART?
TRUTH BE TOLD, I DON'T KNOW MUCH ABOUT ART.
I'D LIKELY WALK INTO THAT GALLERY AND FEEL LIKE I DON'T UNDERSTAND ANYTHING.
I MEAN, I'M SURE YOUR STUFF IS INCREDIBLE. I JUST MEANT ***ANY*** ART.
I LIKE ART, I JUST DIDN'T DO ALL THAT WELL IN SCHOOL.
THAT'S OKAY. AT LEAST YOU DON'T PRETEND TO KNOW WHAT YOU'RE TALKING ABOUT. THAT'S ALWAYS FAKE AND BORING. AND ACCORDING TO THE ART WORLD, THAT'S A CARDINAL SIN.
IF THE ARTWORK IS FAKE AND IT BORES YOU.
YOU SEEM REAL.
THANK YOU, MISS.
I'M GOING TO BET YOUR SHOW WILL BE ANYTHING BUT BORING.

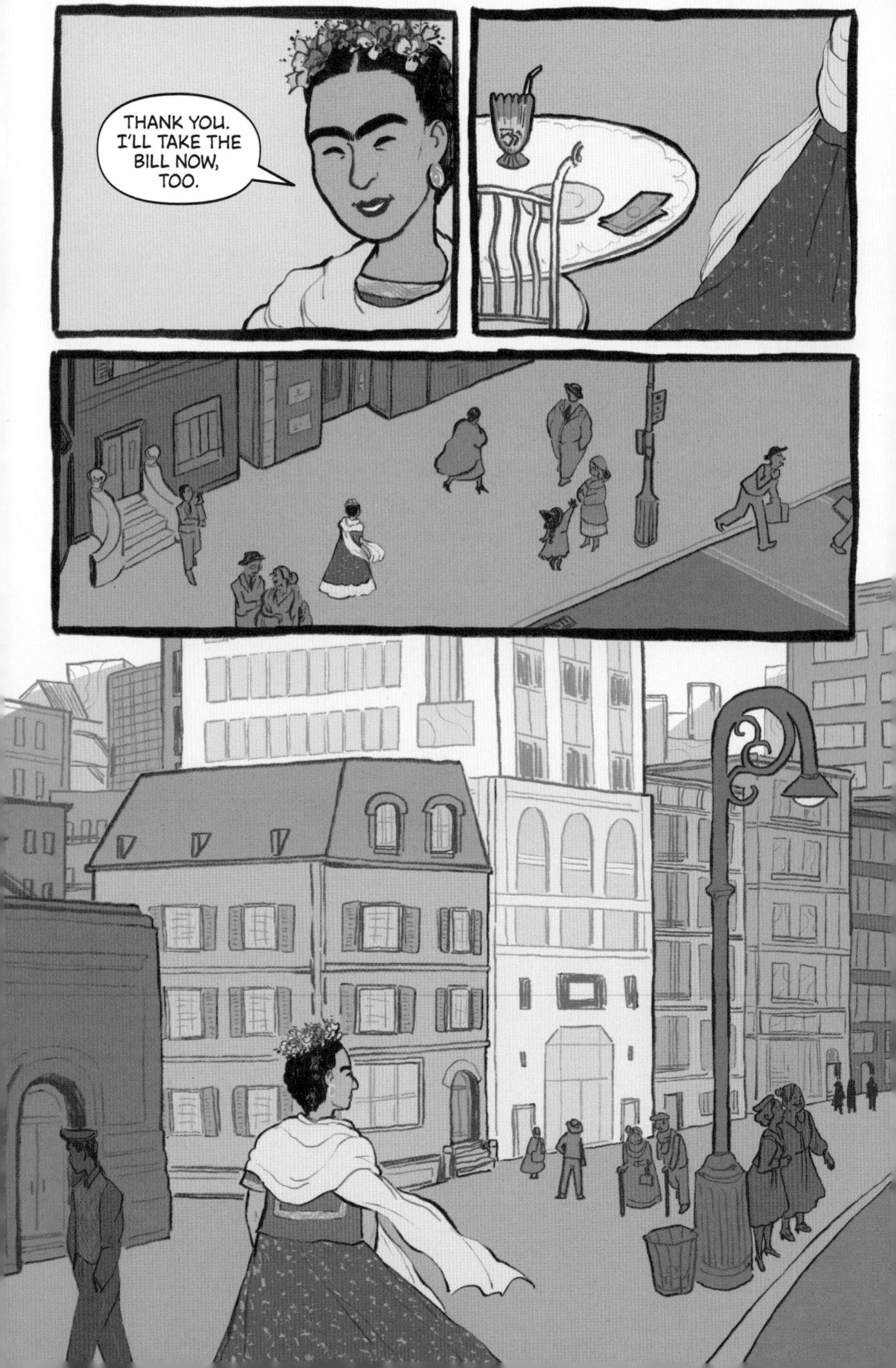
THANK YOU. I'LL TAKE THE BILL NOW, TOO.

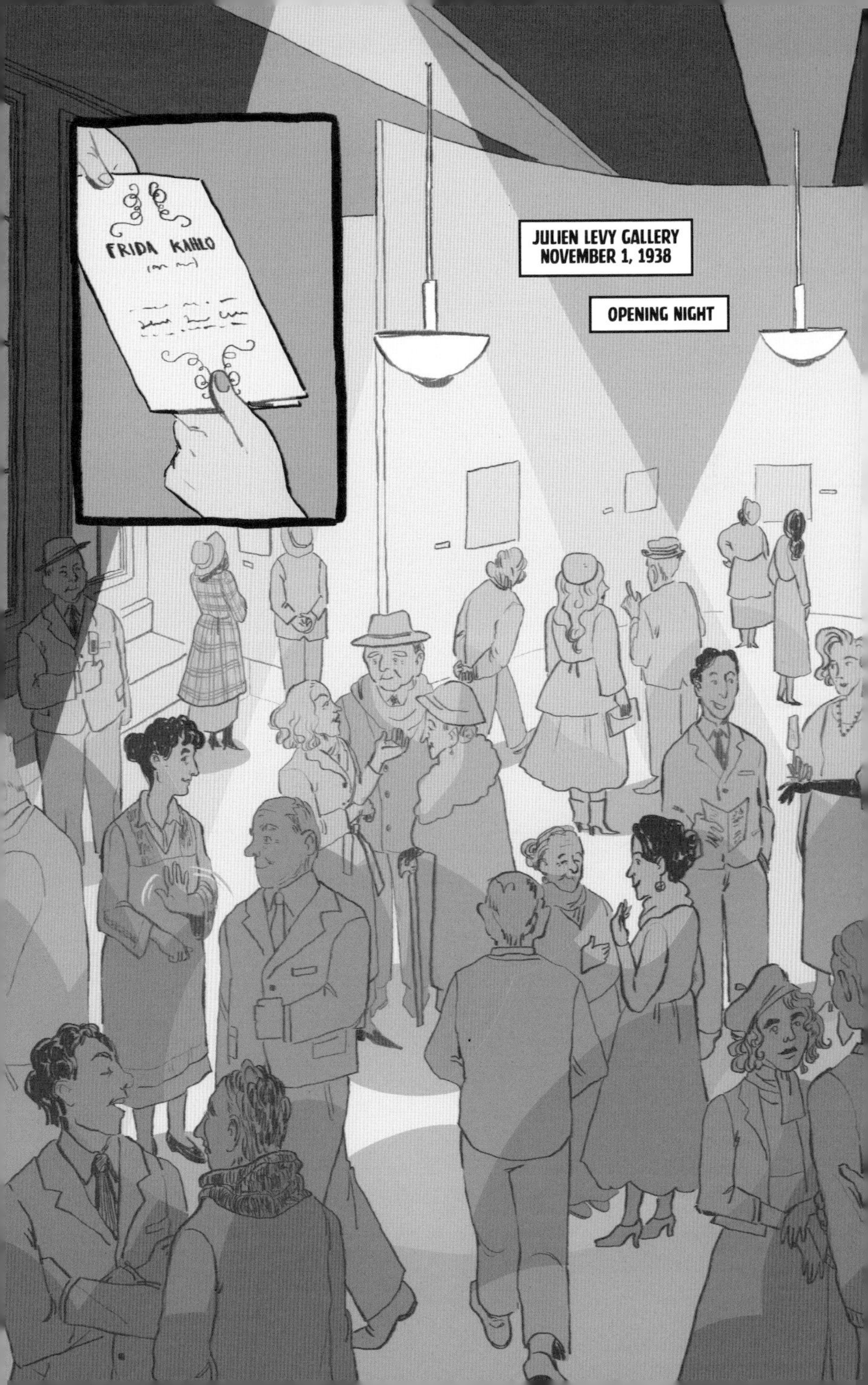
FRIDA KAHLO
JULIEN LEVY GALLERY
NOVEMBER 1, 1938
OPENING NIGHT

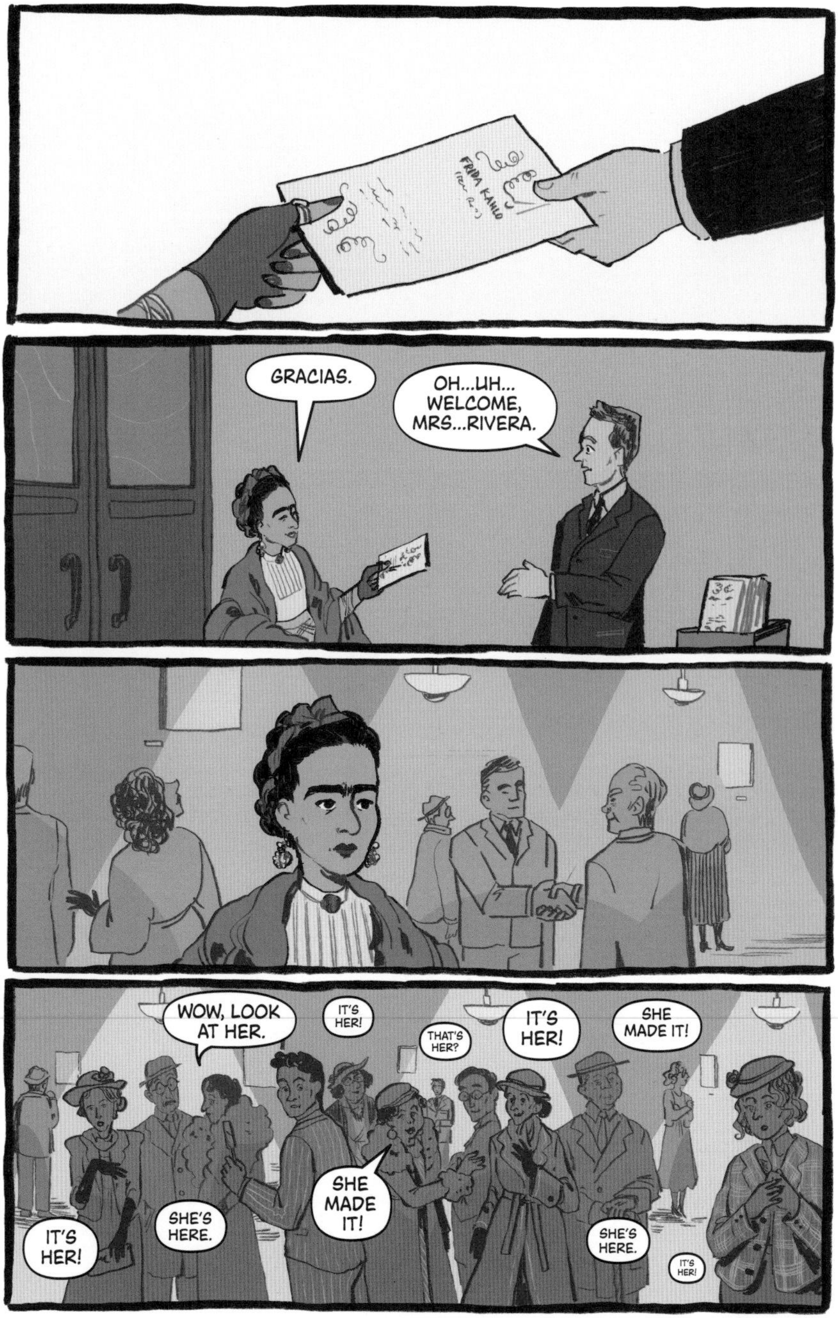
FRIDA KAHLO
GRACIAS.
OH...UH... WELCOME, MRS...RIVERA.
WOW, LOOK AT HER.
IT'S HER!
THAT'S HER?
IT'S HER!
SHE MADE IT!
IT'S HER!
SHE'S HERE.
SHE MADE IT!
SHE'S HERE.
IT'S HER!

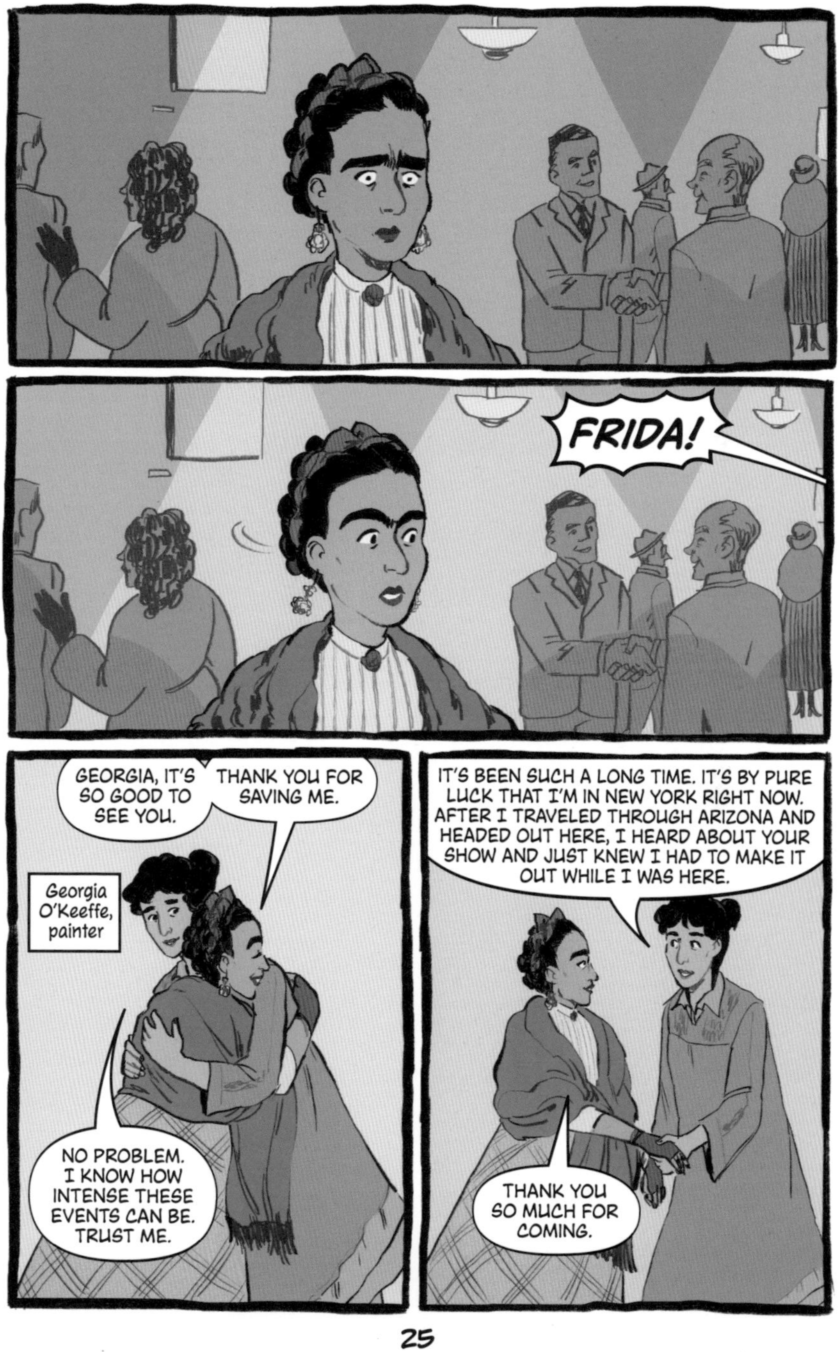
FRIDA!
GEORGIA, IT'S SO GOOD TO SEE YOU.
THANK YOU FOR SAVING ME.
Georgia O'Keeffe, painter
NO PROBLEM. I KNOW HOW INTENSE THESE EVENTS CAN BE. TRUST ME.
IT'S BEEN SUCH A LONG TIME. IT'S BY PURE LUCK THAT I'M IN NEW YORK RIGHT NOW. AFTER I TRAVELED THROUGH ARIZONA AND HEADED OUT HERE, I HEARD ABOUT YOUR SHOW AND JUST KNEW I HAD TO MAKE IT OUT WHILE I WAS HERE.
THANK YOU SO MUCH FOR COMING.

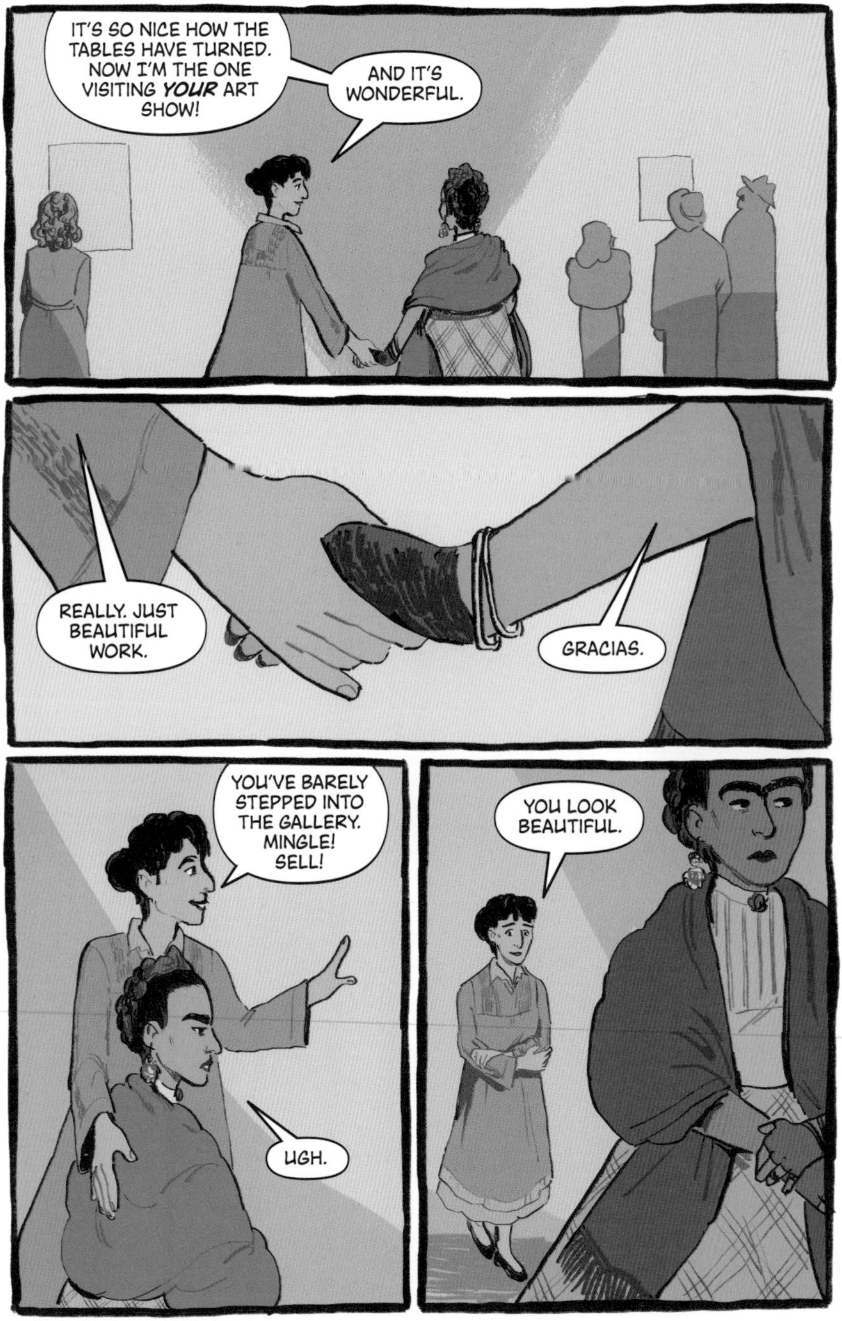
IT'S SO NICE HOW THE TABLES HAVE TURNED. NOW I'M THE ONE VISITING *YOUR* ART SHOW!
AND IT'S WONDERFUL.
REALLY. JUST BEAUTIFUL WORK.
GRACIAS.
YOU'VE BARELY STEPPED INTO THE GALLERY. MINGLE! SELL!
UGH.
YOU LOOK BEAUTIFUL.

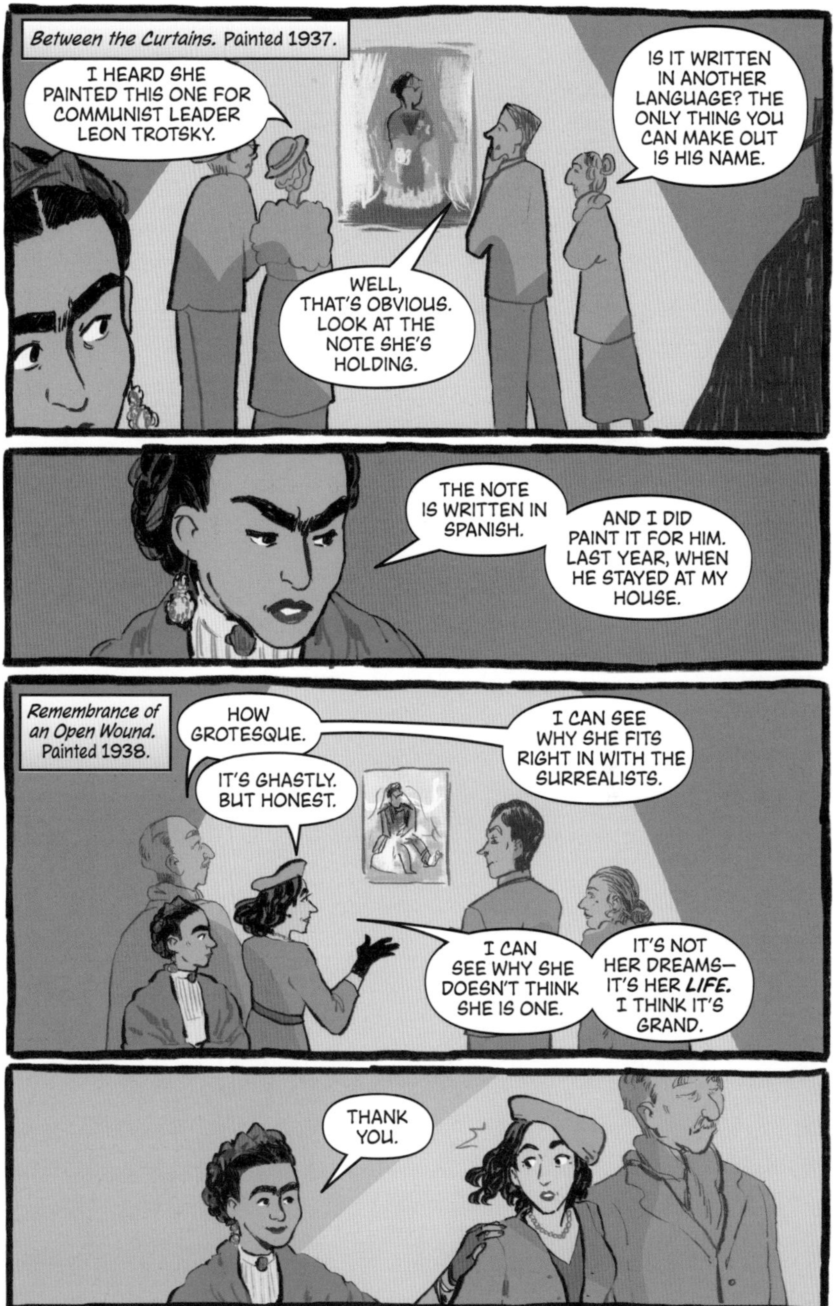
Between the Curtains. Painted 1937.
I HEARD SHE PAINTED THIS ONE FOR COMMUNIST LEADER LEON TROTSKY.
IS IT WRITTEN IN ANOTHER LANGUAGE? THE ONLY THING YOU CAN MAKE OUT IS HIS NAME.
WELL, THAT'S OBVIOUS. LOOK AT THE NOTE SHE'S HOLDING.
THE NOTE IS WRITTEN IN SPANISH.
AND I DID PAINT IT FOR HIM. LAST YEAR, WHEN HE STAYED AT MY HOUSE.
Remembrance of an Open Wound. Painted 1938.
HOW GROTESQUE.
I CAN SEE WHY SHE FITS RIGHT IN WITH THE SURREALISTS.
IT'S GHASTLY. BUT HONEST.
I CAN SEE WHY SHE DOESN'T THINK SHE IS ONE.
IT'S NOT HER DREAMS— IT'S HER LIFE. I THINK IT'S GRAND.
THANK YOU.

Surrealism

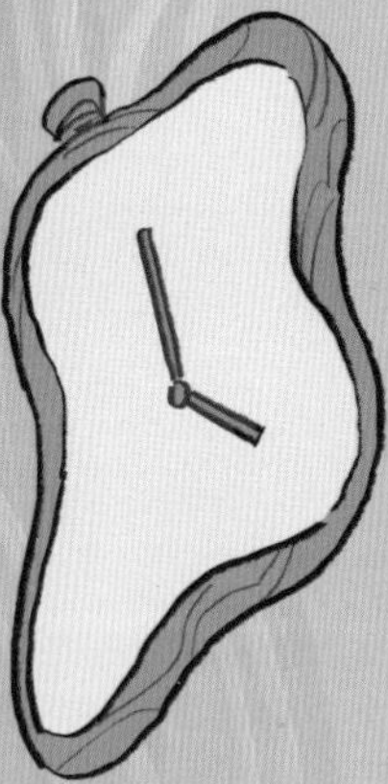

Surrealism was a twentieth-century artistic and cultural movement led by French writer André Breton that became popular in Europe after World War I. This form of expression aimed to discover the world through fantasy and dreamlike, subconscious states, as opposed to through logical thought.

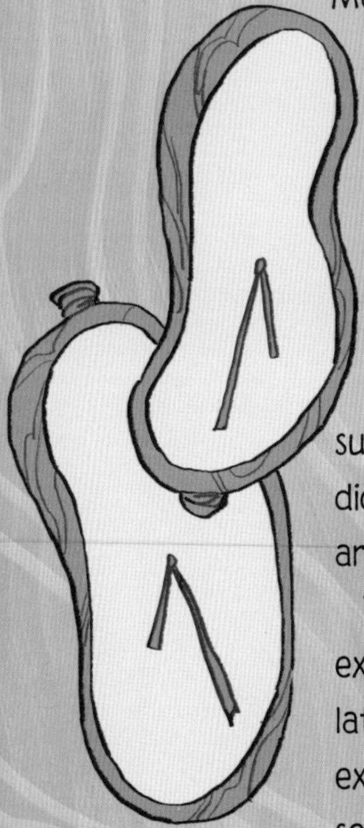

The movement included many well-known artists, writers, and thinkers, such as René Magritte, Max Ernst, Dorothea Tanning, Leonora Carrington, and most famously, Salvador Dalí. In fact, Dalí's painting *The Persistence of Memory*, which features melted clocks that are draped over mysterious objects in a dark, gloomy landscape, is considered one of the most famous works of surrealism. While Frida Kahlo did not consider herself a surrealist painter, many others in the art world did, simply because she rose to prominence around the same time.

The success of surrealism, and its ability to explore dreams and the human mind, influenced later artistic movements including abstract expressionism and pop art. Surrealism is widely seen in modern music, art, and literature.

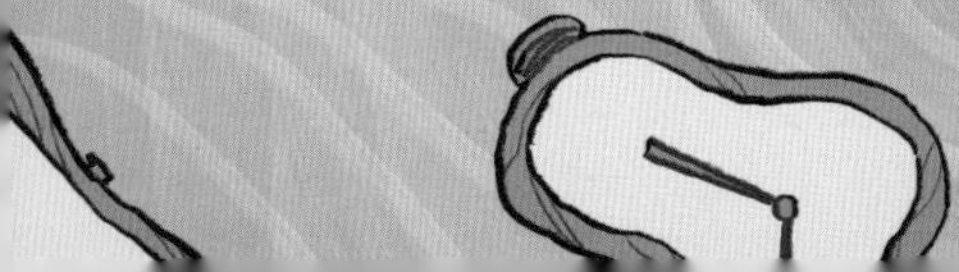

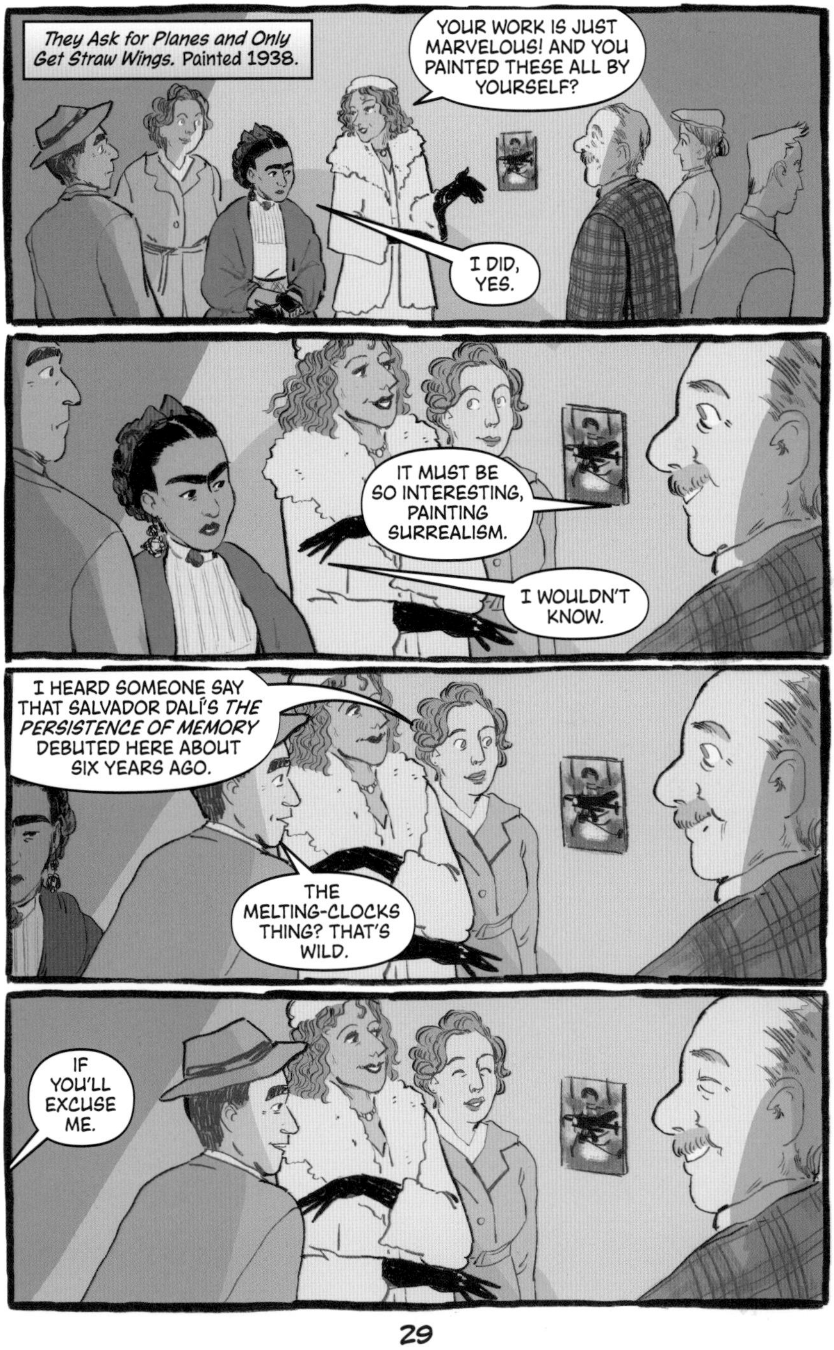

They Ask for Planes and Only Get Straw Wings. Painted 1938.
YOUR WORK IS JUST MARVELOUS! AND YOU PAINTED THESE ALL BY YOURSELF?
I DID, YES.
IT MUST BE SO INTERESTING, PAINTING SURREALISM.
I WOULDN'T KNOW.
I HEARD SOMEONE SAY THAT SALVADOR DALÍ'S *THE PERSISTENCE OF MEMORY* DEBUTED HERE ABOUT SIX YEARS AGO.
THE MELTING-CLOCKS THING? THAT'S WILD.
IF YOU'LL EXCUSE ME.

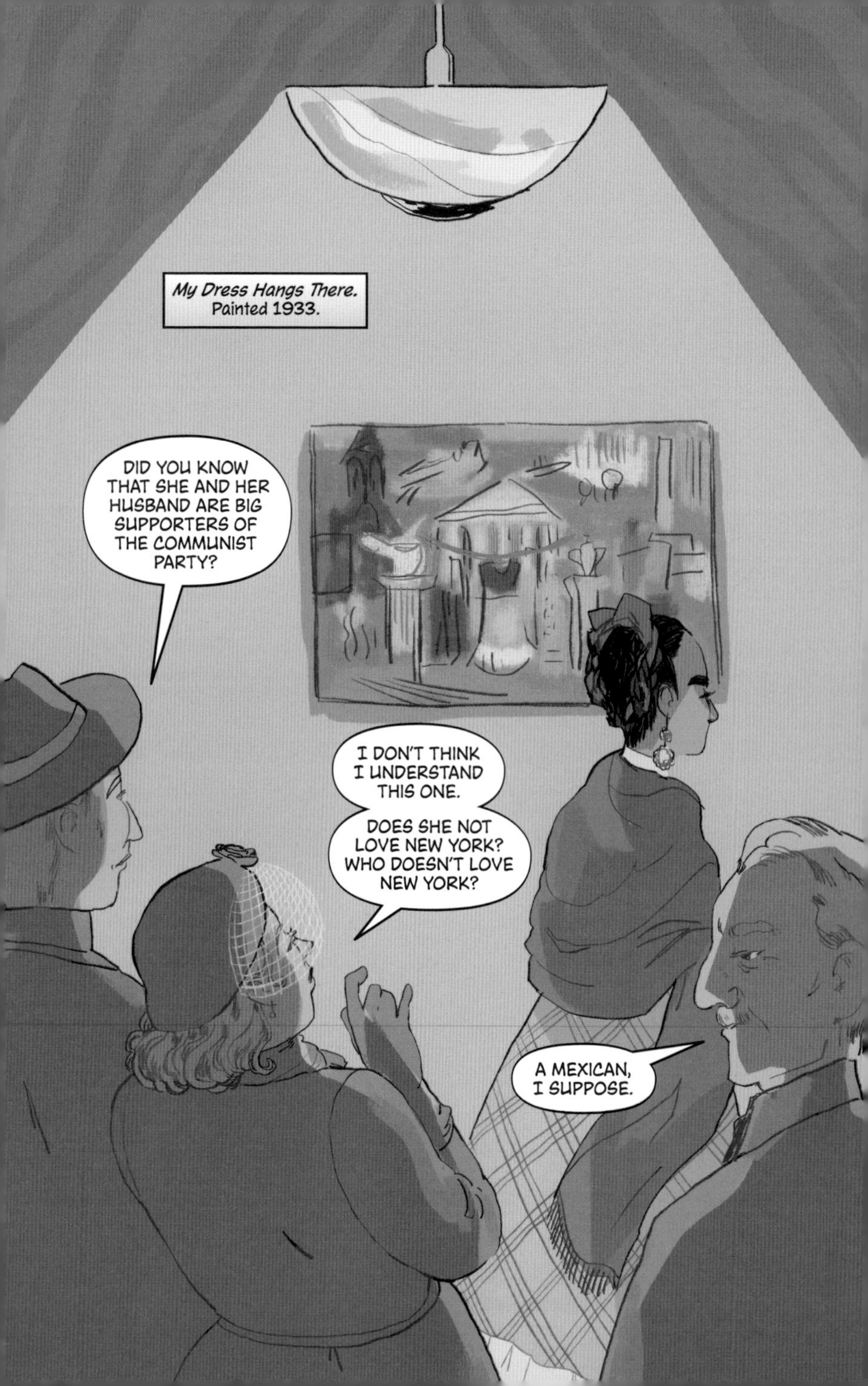
My Dress Hangs There. Painted 1933.
DID YOU KNOW THAT SHE AND HER HUSBAND ARE BIG SUPPORTERS OF THE COMMUNIST PARTY?
I DON'T THINK I UNDERSTAND THIS ONE.
DOES SHE NOT LOVE NEW YORK? WHO DOESN'T LOVE NEW YORK?
A MEXICAN, I SUPPOSE.

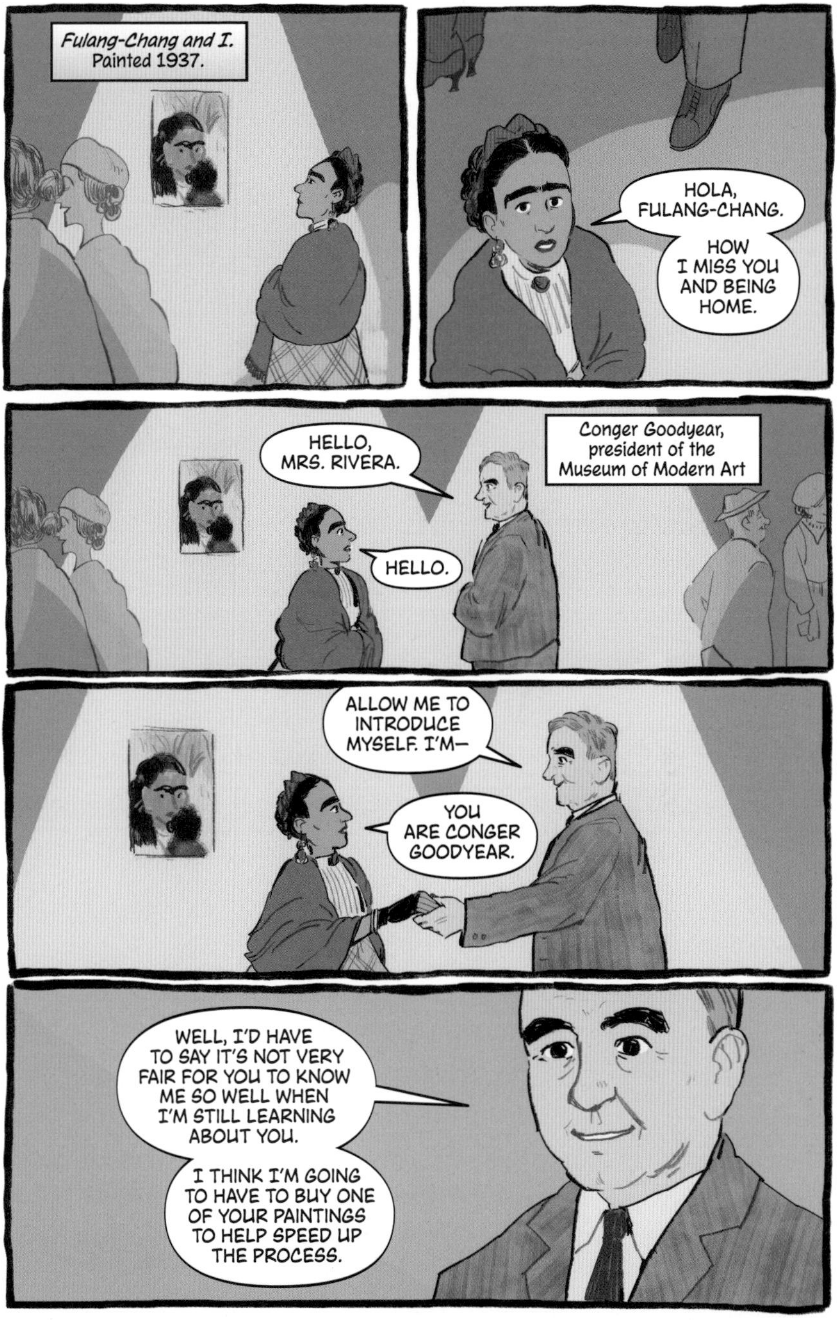

Fulang-Chang and I. Painted 1937.
HOLA, FULANG-CHANG.
HOW I MISS YOU AND BEING HOME.
HELLO, MRS. RIVERA.
Conger Goodyear, president of the Museum of Modern Art
HELLO.
ALLOW ME TO INTRODUCE MYSELF. I'M—
YOU ARE CONGER GOODYEAR.
WELL, I'D HAVE TO SAY IT'S NOT VERY FAIR FOR YOU TO KNOW ME SO WELL WHEN I'M STILL LEARNING ABOUT YOU.
I THINK I'M GOING TO HAVE TO BUY ONE OF YOUR PAINTINGS TO HELP SPEED UP THE PROCESS.

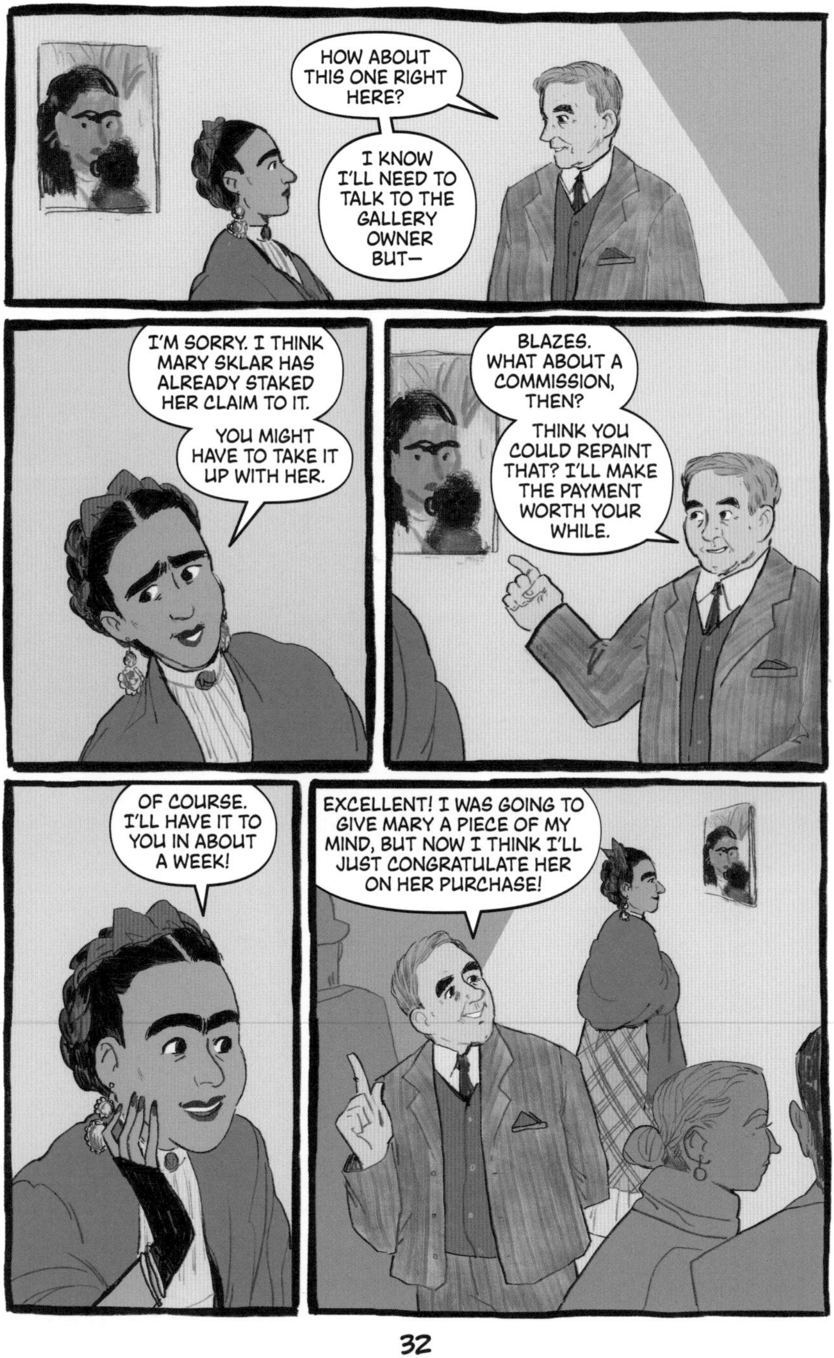
HOW ABOUT THIS ONE RIGHT HERE?
I KNOW I'LL NEED TO TALK TO THE GALLERY OWNER BUT—
I'M SORRY. I THINK MARY SKLAR HAS ALREADY STAKED HER CLAIM TO IT.
YOU MIGHT HAVE TO TAKE IT UP WITH HER.
BLAZES. WHAT ABOUT A COMMISSION, THEN?
THINK YOU COULD REPAINT THAT? I'LL MAKE THE PAYMENT WORTH YOUR WHILE.
OF COURSE. I'LL HAVE IT TO YOU IN ABOUT A WEEK!
EXCELLENT! I WAS GOING TO GIVE MARY A PIECE OF MY MIND, BUT NOW I THINK I'LL JUST CONGRATULATE HER ON HER PURCHASE!

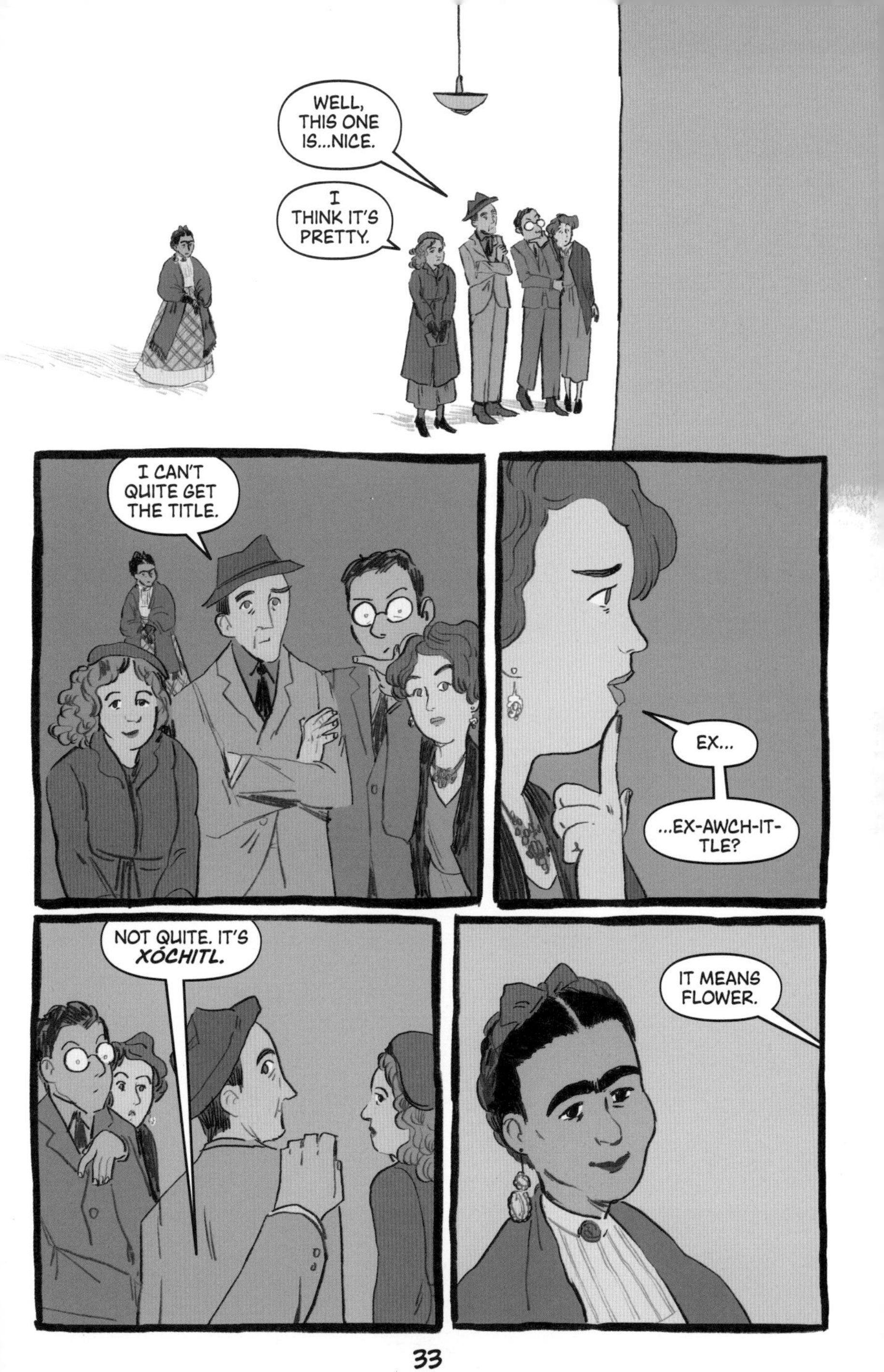

WELL, THIS ONE IS...NICE.
I THINK IT'S PRETTY.
I CAN'T QUITE GET THE TITLE.
EX...
...EX-AWCH-IT-TLE?
NOT QUITE. IT'S XÓCHITL.
IT MEANS FLOWER.

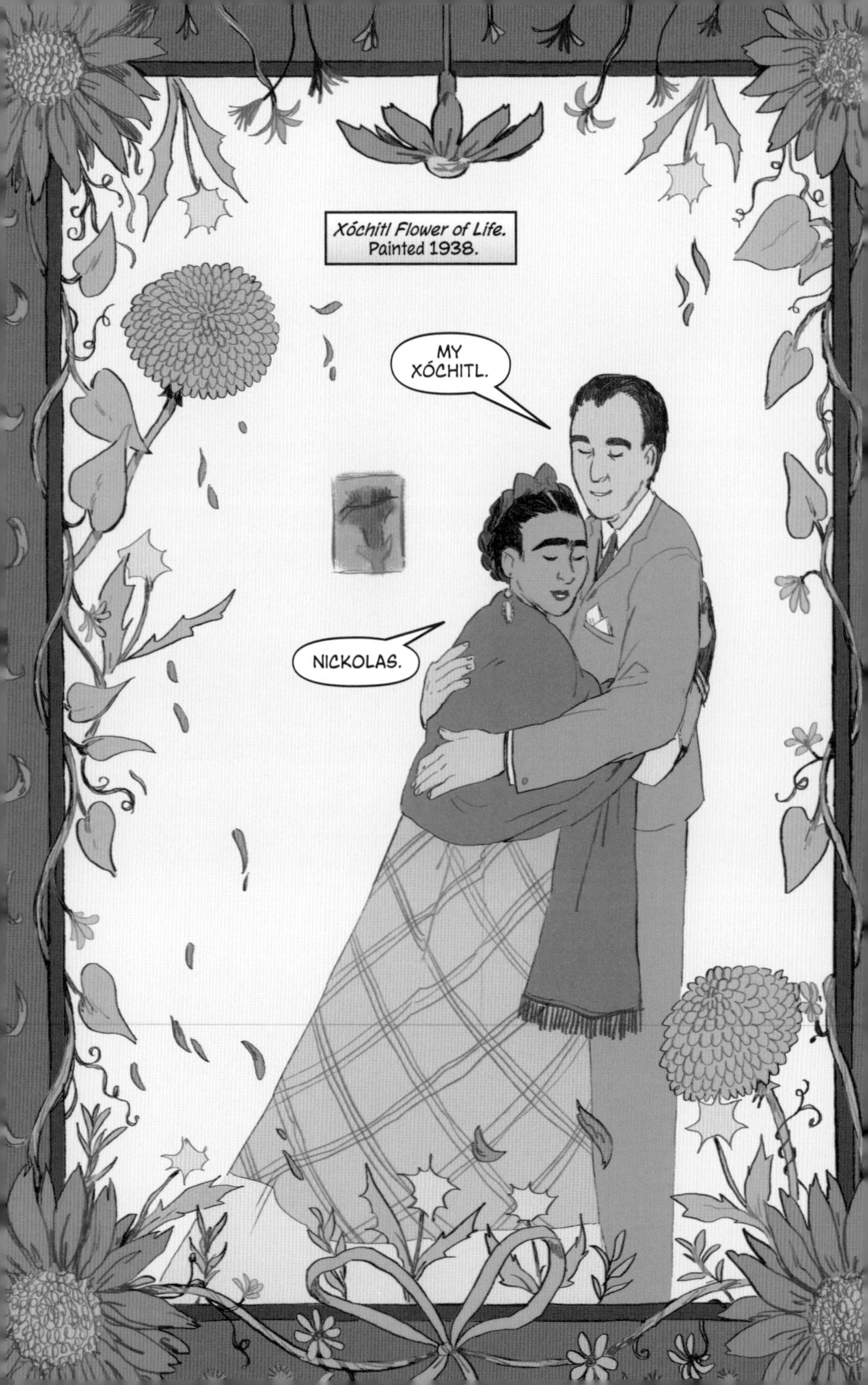
Xóchitl Flower of Life. Painted 1938.
MY XÓCHITL.
NICKOLAS.

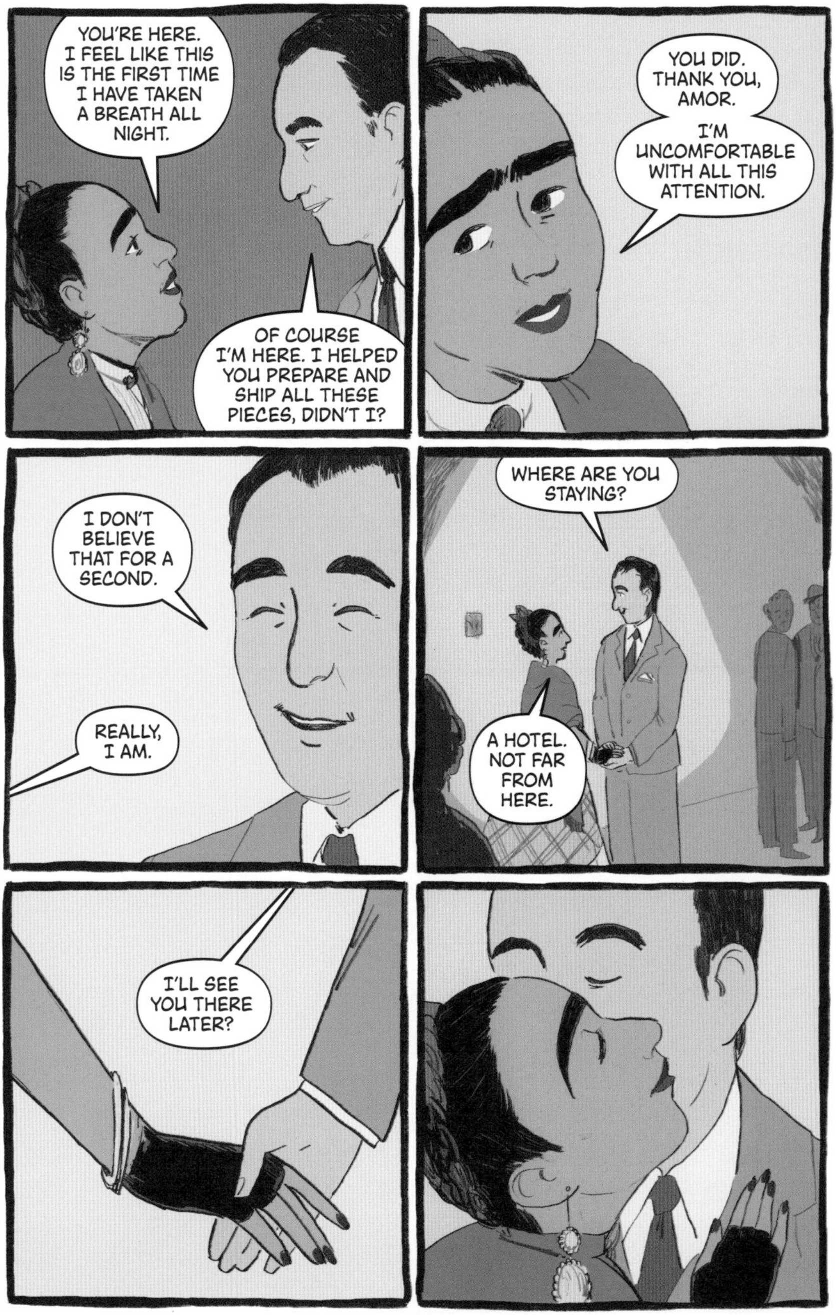
YOU'RE HERE. I FEEL LIKE THIS IS THE FIRST TIME I HAVE TAKEN A BREATH ALL NIGHT.
OF COURSE I'M HERE. I HELPED YOU PREPARE AND SHIP ALL THESE PIECES, DIDN'T I?
YOU DID. THANK YOU, AMOR.
I'M UNCOMFORTABLE WITH ALL THIS ATTENTION.
I DON'T BELIEVE THAT FOR A SECOND.
REALLY, I AM.
WHERE ARE YOU STAYING?
A HOTEL. NOT FAR FROM HERE.
I'LL SEE YOU THERE LATER?

Nickolas Muray

Nickolas Muray was born Miklós Mandl in Szeged, Hungary, on February 15, 1892. When he was two years old, his family moved to Budapest, where he developed a love for art and photography.

In 1913, Nickolas moved to New York and found work in Brooklyn as a color printer. By 1920, Nickolas opened up a photography studio in Greenwich Village so he could take more portraits. This led to *Harper's Bazaar* commissioning him to take a photograph of Broadway actress Florence Reed, and not long after, Nickolas went on to photograph for *Vanity Fair*, *Ladies' Home Journal*, *Vogue*, and the *New York Times*. Between 1920 and 1940, he took over ten thousand portraits.

Nickolas was also a skilled fencer, competing in the saber fencing events at the 1928 and 1932 Summer Olympics. He won many awards and championships during his fencing career, including the US National Saber Team Championship and the Metropolitan Saber Fencing Championship. On November 2, 1965, he suffered a heart attack while fencing at the New York Athletic Club. He died at the age of seventy-three.

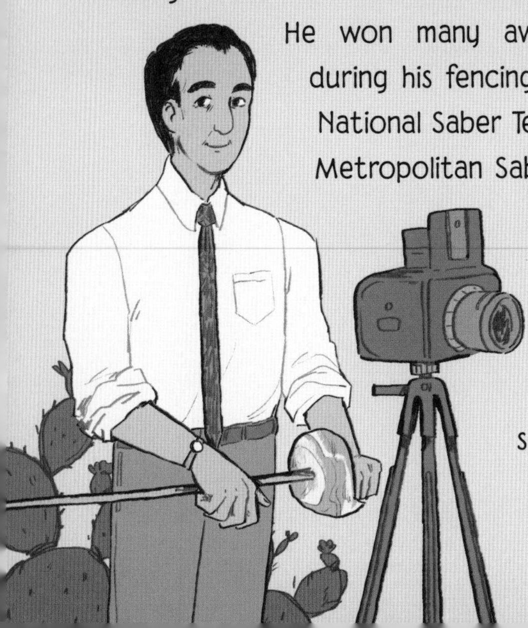

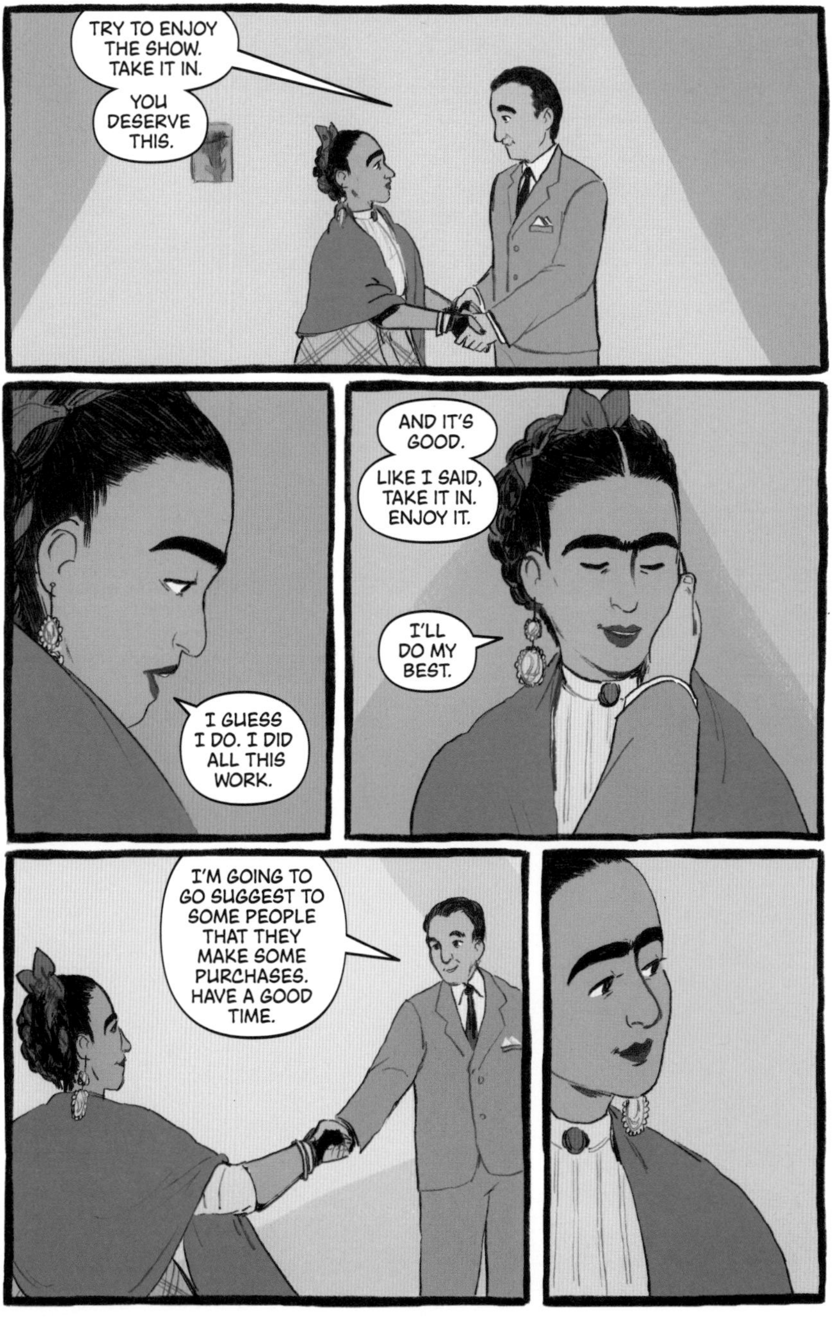
TRY TO ENJOY THE SHOW. TAKE IT IN.
YOU DESERVE THIS.
I GUESS I DO. I DID ALL THIS WORK.
AND IT'S GOOD.
LIKE I SAID, TAKE IT IN. ENJOY IT.
I'LL DO MY BEST.
I'M GOING TO GO SUGGEST TO SOME PEOPLE THAT THEY MAKE SOME PURCHASES. HAVE A GOOD TIME.

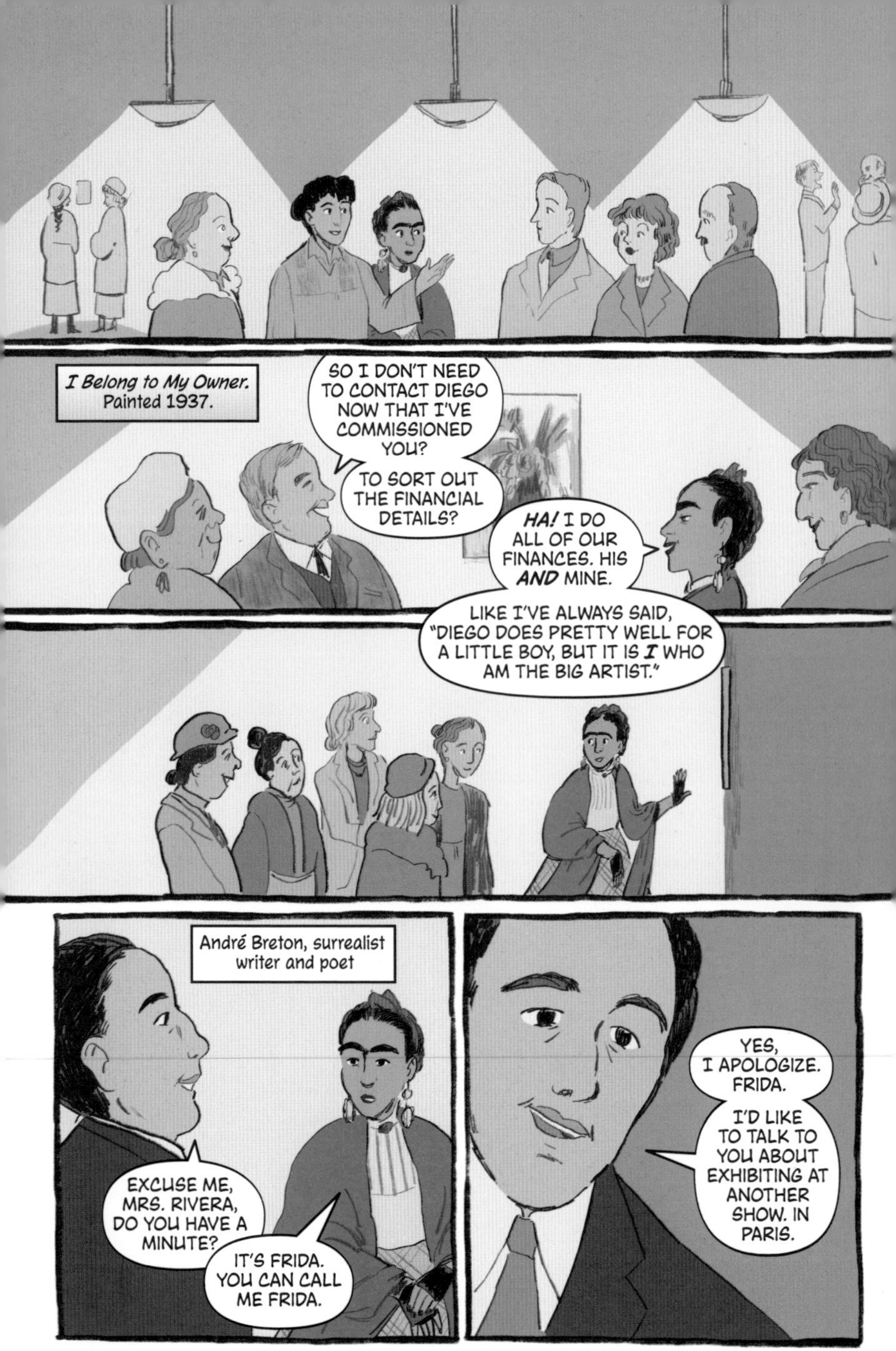
I Belong to My Owner. Painted 1937.
SO I DON'T NEED TO CONTACT DIEGO NOW THAT I'VE COMMISSIONED YOU?
TO SORT OUT THE FINANCIAL DETAILS?
HA! I DO ALL OF OUR FINANCES. HIS ***AND*** MINE.
LIKE I'VE ALWAYS SAID, "DIEGO DOES PRETTY WELL FOR A LITTLE BOY, BUT IT IS ***I*** WHO AM THE BIG ARTIST."
André Breton, surrealist writer and poet
EXCUSE ME, MRS. RIVERA, DO YOU HAVE A MINUTE?
IT'S FRIDA. YOU CAN CALL ME FRIDA.
YES, I APOLOGIZE. FRIDA.
I'D LIKE TO TALK TO YOU ABOUT EXHIBITING AT ANOTHER SHOW. IN PARIS.

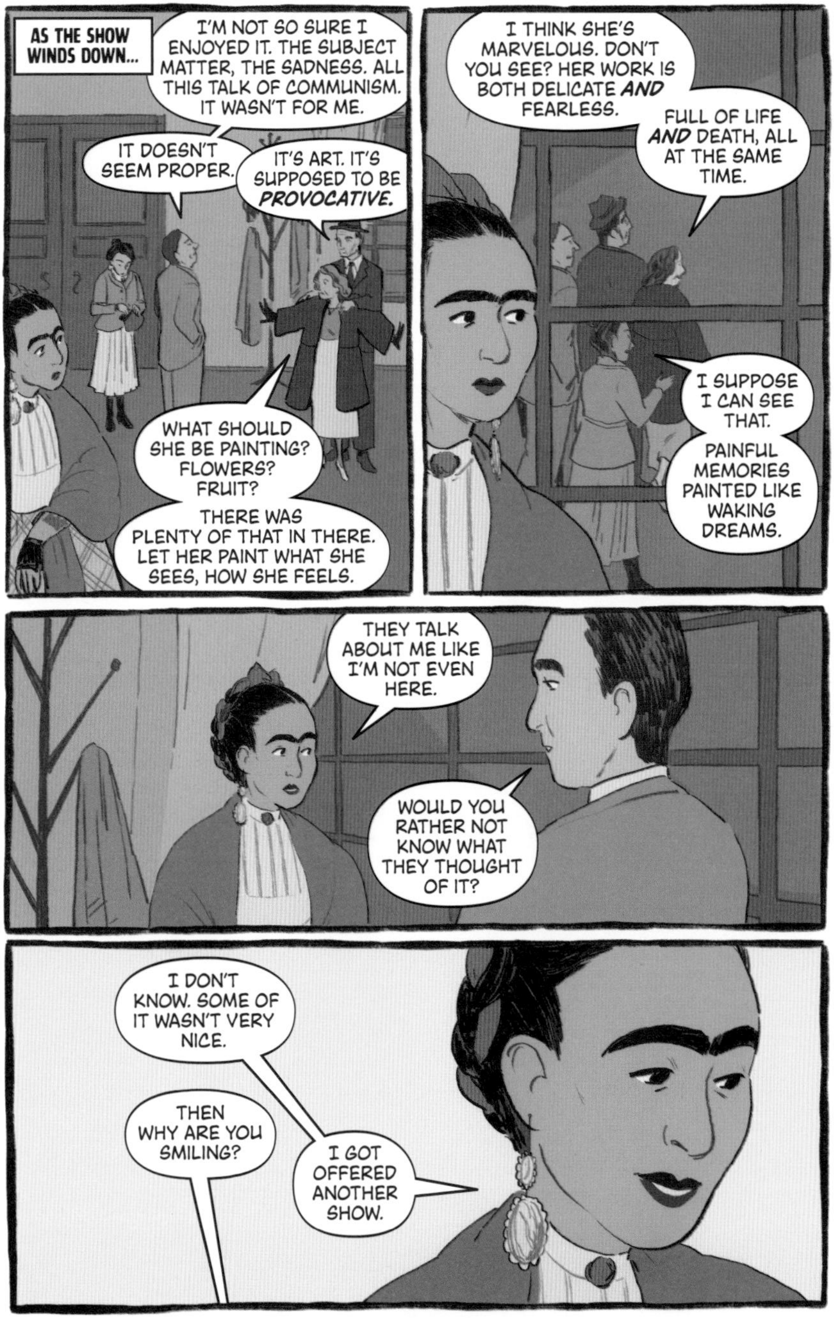
AS THE SHOW WINDS DOWN...
I'M NOT SO SURE I ENJOYED IT. THE SUBJECT MATTER, THE SADNESS. ALL THIS TALK OF COMMUNISM. IT WASN'T FOR ME.
IT DOESN'T SEEM PROPER.
IT'S ART. IT'S SUPPOSED TO BE *PROVOCATIVE.*
WHAT SHOULD SHE BE PAINTING? FLOWERS? FRUIT?
THERE WAS PLENTY OF THAT IN THERE. LET HER PAINT WHAT SHE SEES, HOW SHE FEELS.
I THINK SHE'S MARVELOUS. DON'T YOU SEE? HER WORK IS BOTH DELICATE ***AND*** FEARLESS.
FULL OF LIFE ***AND*** DEATH, ALL AT THE SAME TIME.
I SUPPOSE I CAN SEE THAT.
PAINFUL MEMORIES PAINTED LIKE WAKING DREAMS.
THEY TALK ABOUT ME LIKE I'M NOT EVEN HERE.
WOULD YOU RATHER NOT KNOW WHAT THEY THOUGHT OF IT?
I DON'T KNOW. SOME OF IT WASN'T VERY NICE.
THEN WHY ARE YOU SMILING?
I GOT OFFERED ANOTHER SHOW.

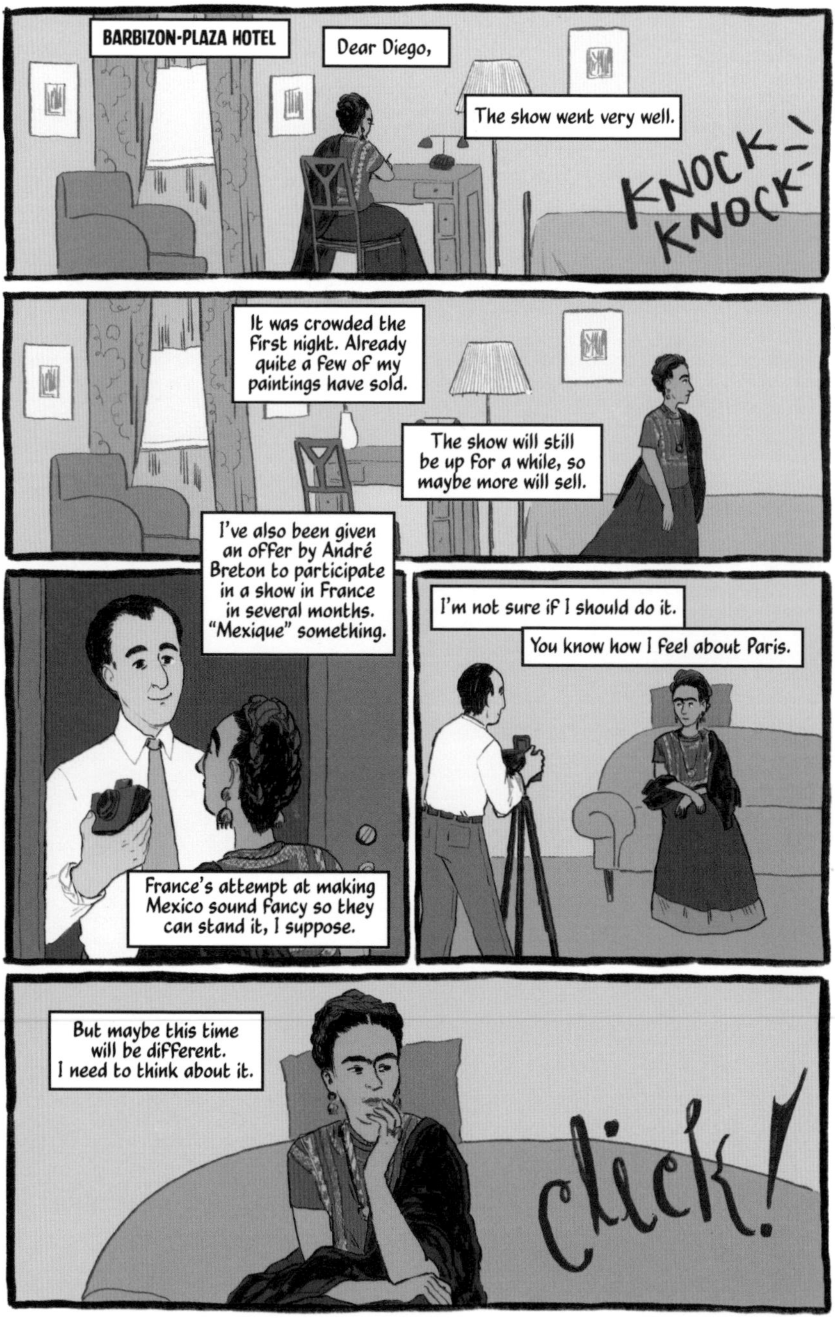
BARBIZON-PLAZA HOTEL
Dear Diego,
The show went very well.
KNOCK KNOCK
It was crowded the first night. Already quite a few of my paintings have sold.
The show will still be up for a while, so maybe more will sell.
I've also been given an offer by André Breton to participate in a show in France in several months. "Mexique" something.
France's attempt at making Mexico sound fancy so they can stand it, I suppose.
I'm not sure if I should do it.
You know how I feel about Paris.
But maybe this time will be different. I need to think about it.
click!

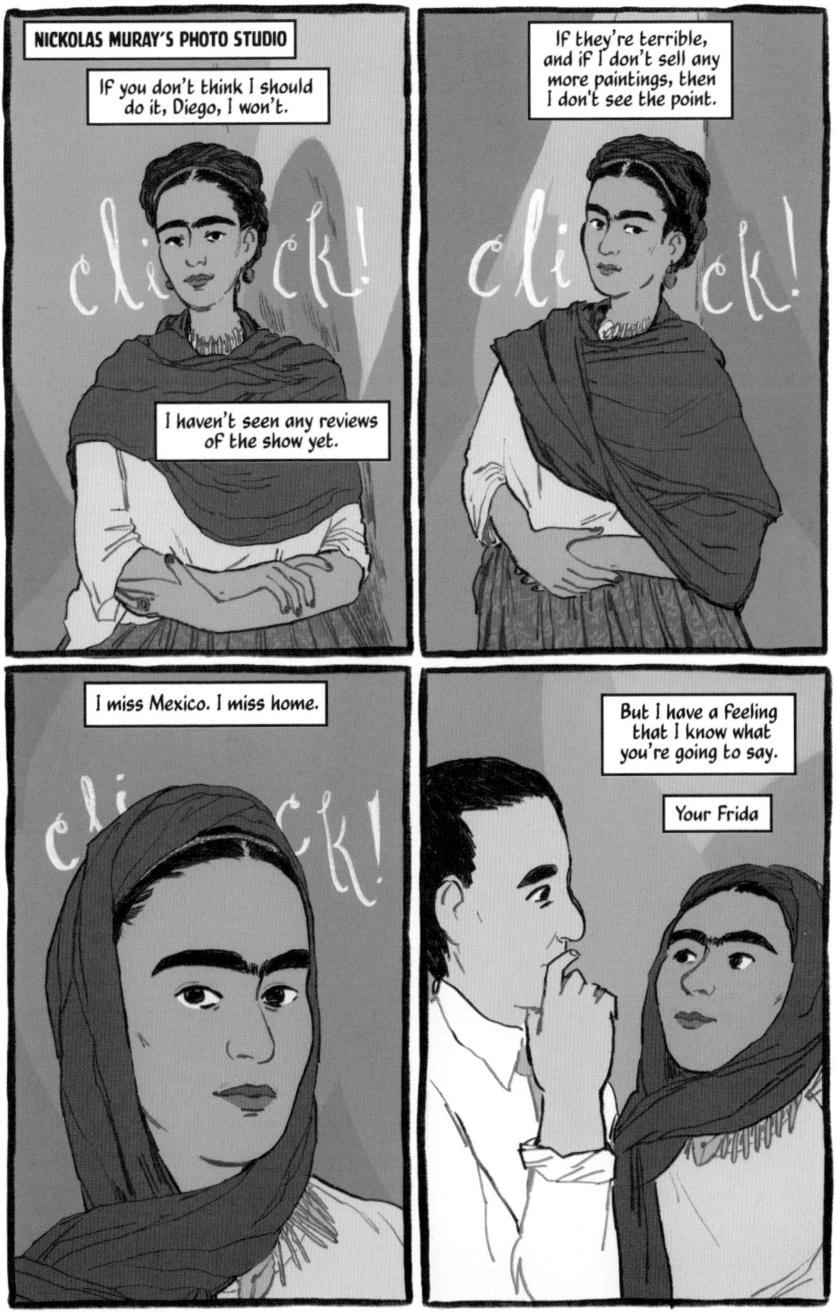
NICKOLAS MURAY'S PHOTO STUDIO
If you don't think I should do it, Diego, I won't.
cli ck!
I haven't seen any reviews of the show yet.
If they're terrible, and if I don't sell any more paintings, then I don't see the point.
cli ck!
I miss Mexico. I miss home.
cli ck!
But I have a feeling that I know what you're going to say.
Your Frida

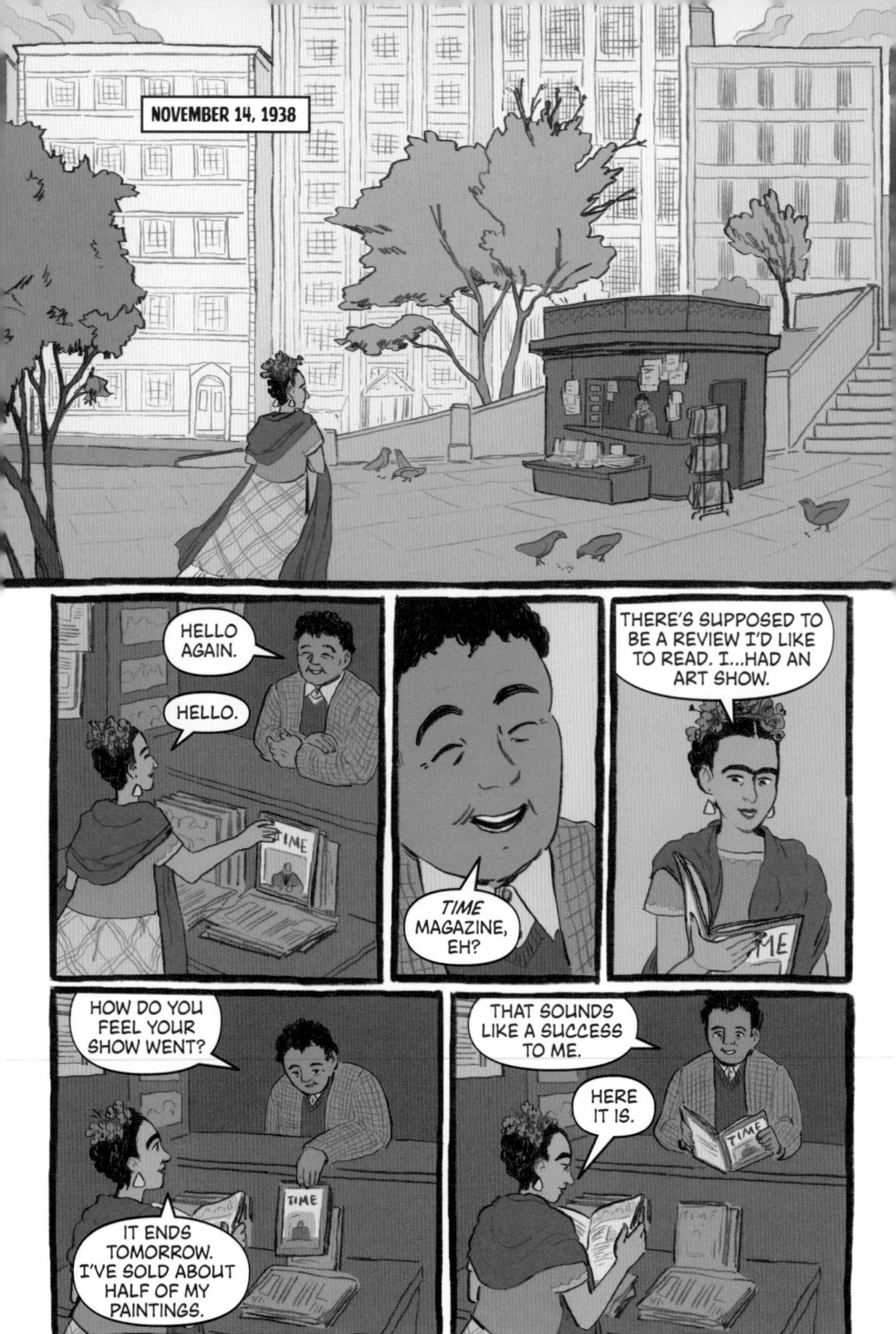
NOVEMBER 14, 1938
HELLO AGAIN.
HELLO.
TIME
TIME MAGAZINE, EH?
THERE'S SUPPOSED TO BE A REVIEW I'D LIKE TO READ. I...HAD AN ART SHOW.
HOW DO YOU FEEL YOUR SHOW WENT?
IT ENDS TOMORROW. I'VE SOLD ABOUT HALF OF MY PAINTINGS.
THAT SOUNDS LIKE A SUCCESS TO ME.
HERE IT IS.

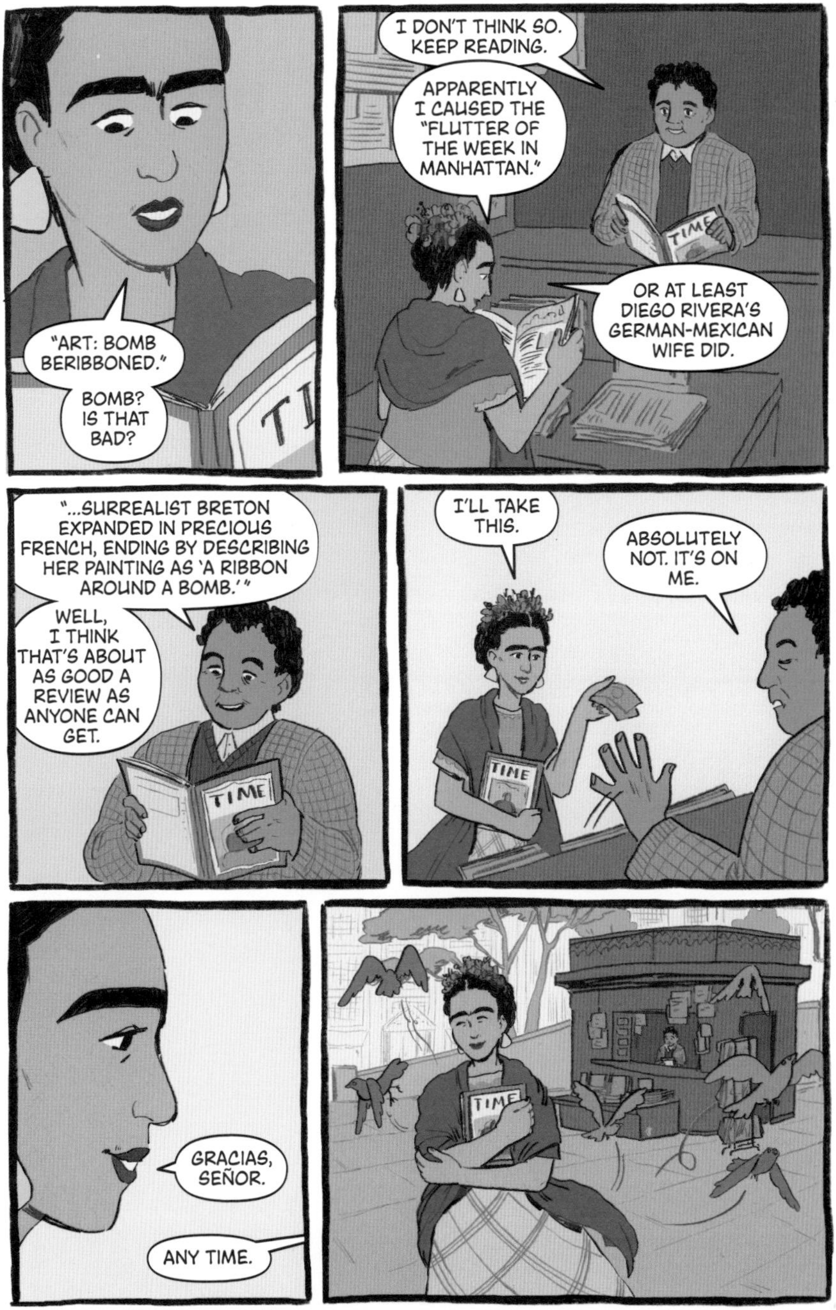
"ART: BOMB BERIBBONED."
BOMB? IS THAT BAD?
I DON'T THINK SO. KEEP READING.
APPARENTLY I CAUSED THE "FLUTTER OF THE WEEK IN MANHATTAN."
OR AT LEAST DIEGO RIVERA'S GERMAN-MEXICAN WIFE DID.
TIME
"...SURREALIST BRETON EXPANDED IN PRECIOUS FRENCH, ENDING BY DESCRIBING HER PAINTING AS 'A RIBBON AROUND A BOMB.'"
WELL, I THINK THAT'S ABOUT AS GOOD A REVIEW AS ANYONE CAN GET.
I'LL TAKE THIS.
ABSOLUTELY NOT. IT'S ON ME.
GRACIAS, SEÑOR.
ANY TIME.

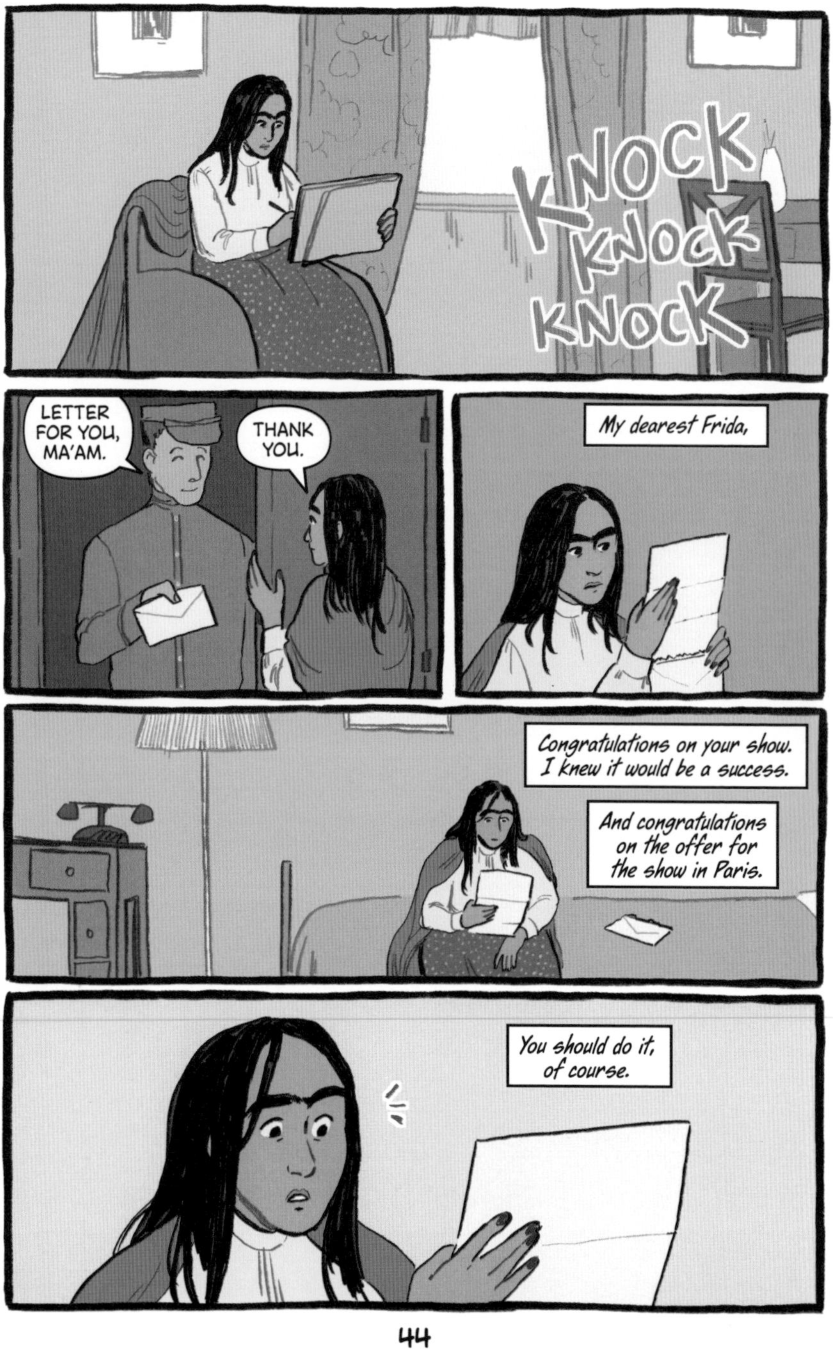
KNOCK
KNOCK
KNOCK
LETTER FOR YOU, MA'AM.
THANK YOU.
My dearest Frida,
Congratulations on your show. I knew it would be a success.
And congratulations on the offer for the show in Paris.
You should do it, of course.

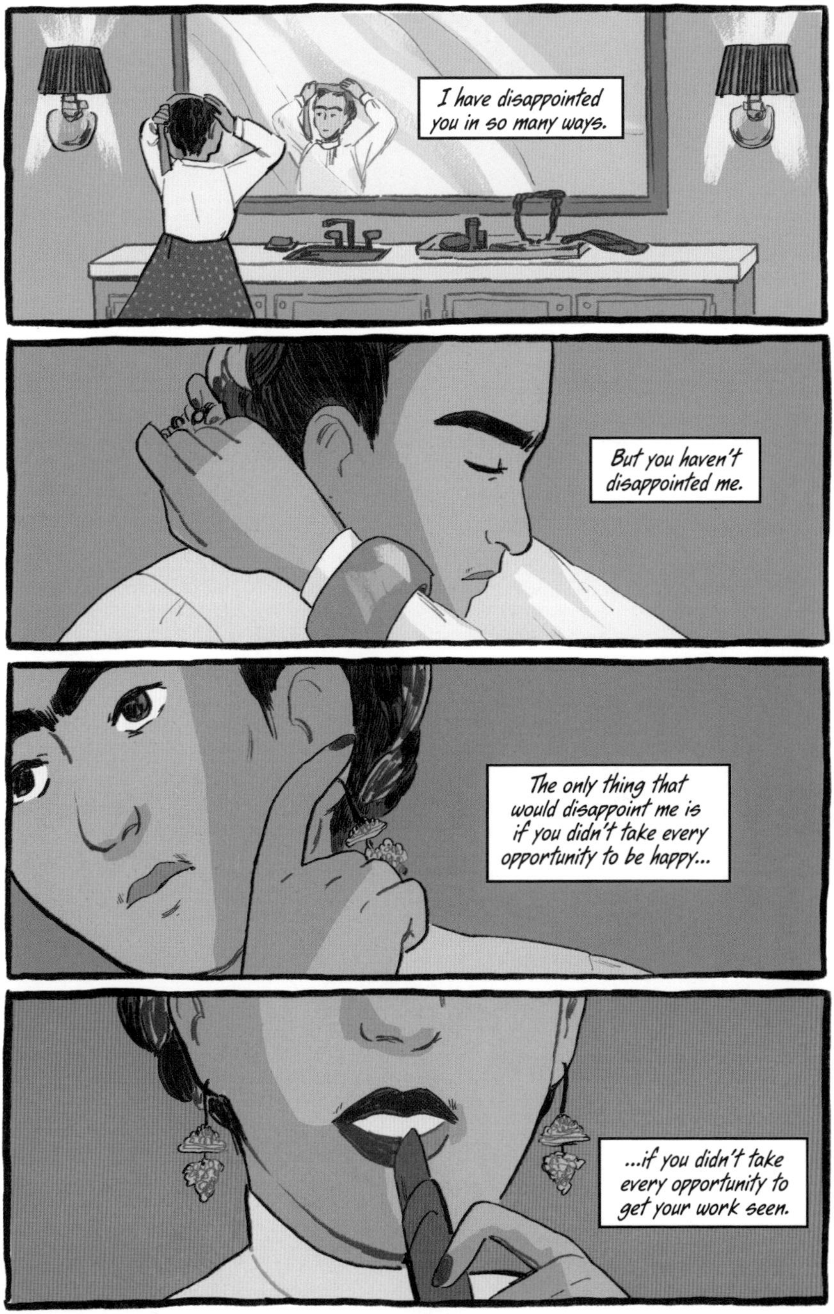
I have disappointed you in so many ways.
But you haven't disappointed me.
The only thing that would disappoint me is if you didn't take every opportunity to be happy...
...if you didn't take every opportunity to get your work seen.

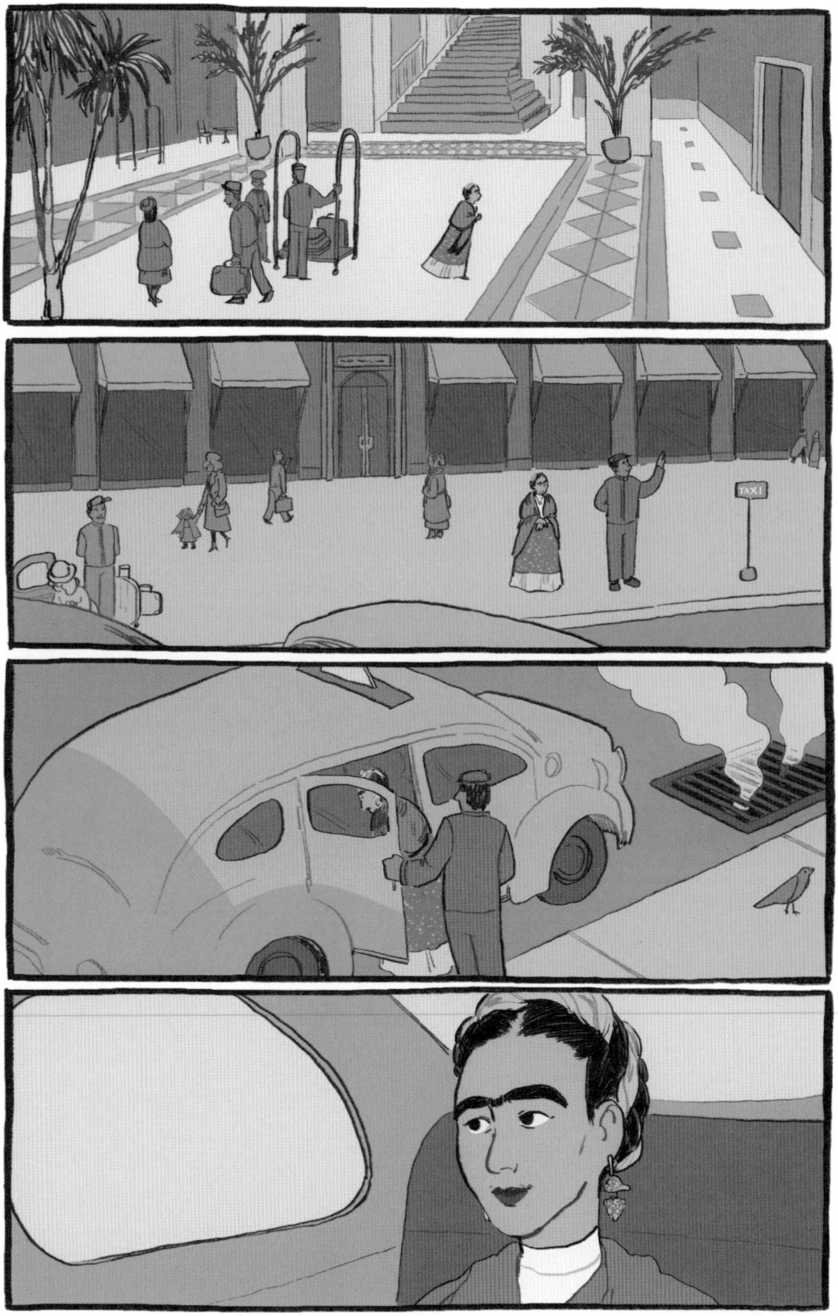
TAXI

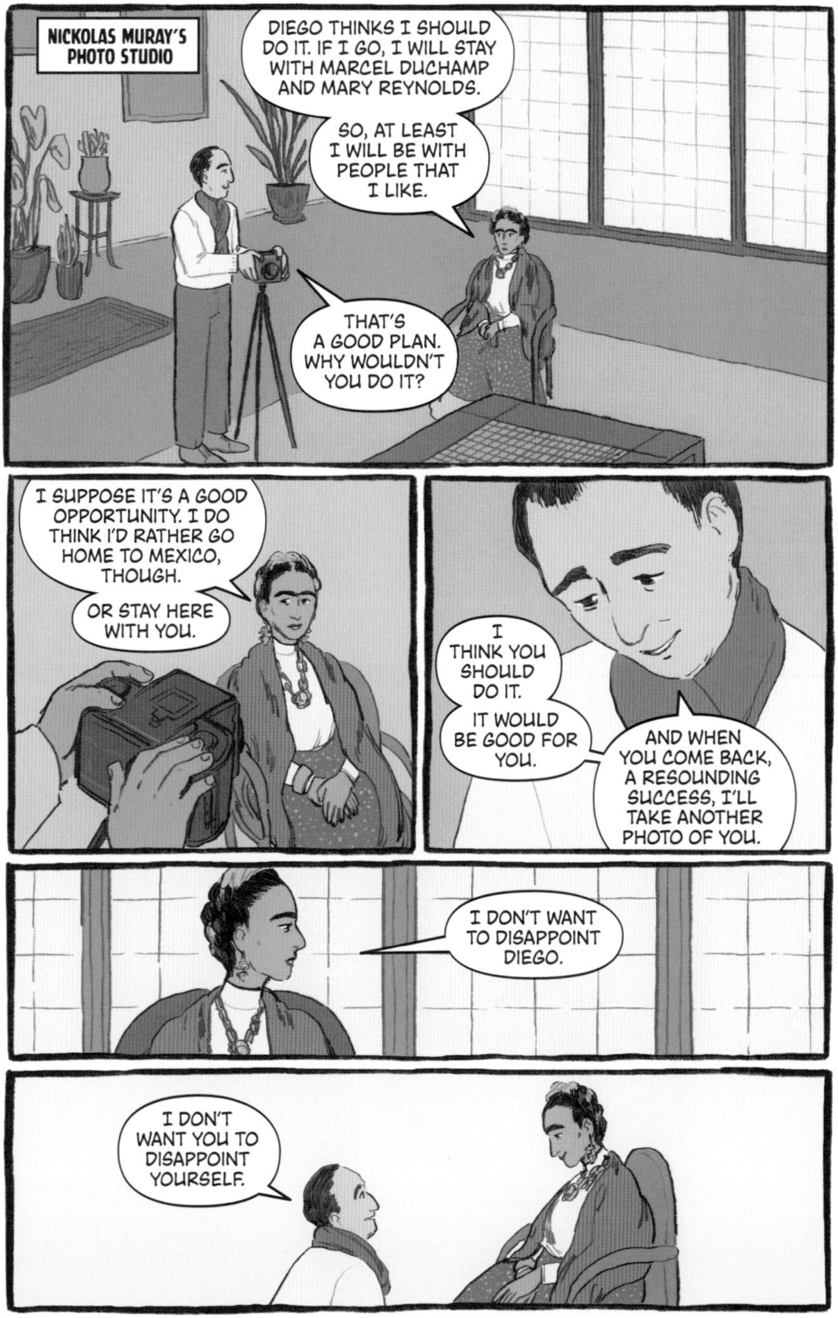
NICKOLAS MURAY'S PHOTO STUDIO
DIEGO THINKS I SHOULD DO IT. IF I GO, I WILL STAY WITH MARCEL DUCHAMP AND MARY REYNOLDS.
SO, AT LEAST I WILL BE WITH PEOPLE THAT I LIKE.
THAT'S A GOOD PLAN. WHY WOULDN'T YOU DO IT?
I SUPPOSE IT'S A GOOD OPPORTUNITY. I DO THINK I'D RATHER GO HOME TO MEXICO, THOUGH.
OR STAY HERE WITH YOU.
I THINK YOU SHOULD DO IT.
IT WOULD BE GOOD FOR YOU.
AND WHEN YOU COME BACK, A RESOUNDING SUCCESS, I'LL TAKE ANOTHER PHOTO OF YOU.
I DON'T WANT TO DISAPPOINT DIEGO.
I DON'T WANT YOU TO DISAPPOINT YOURSELF.

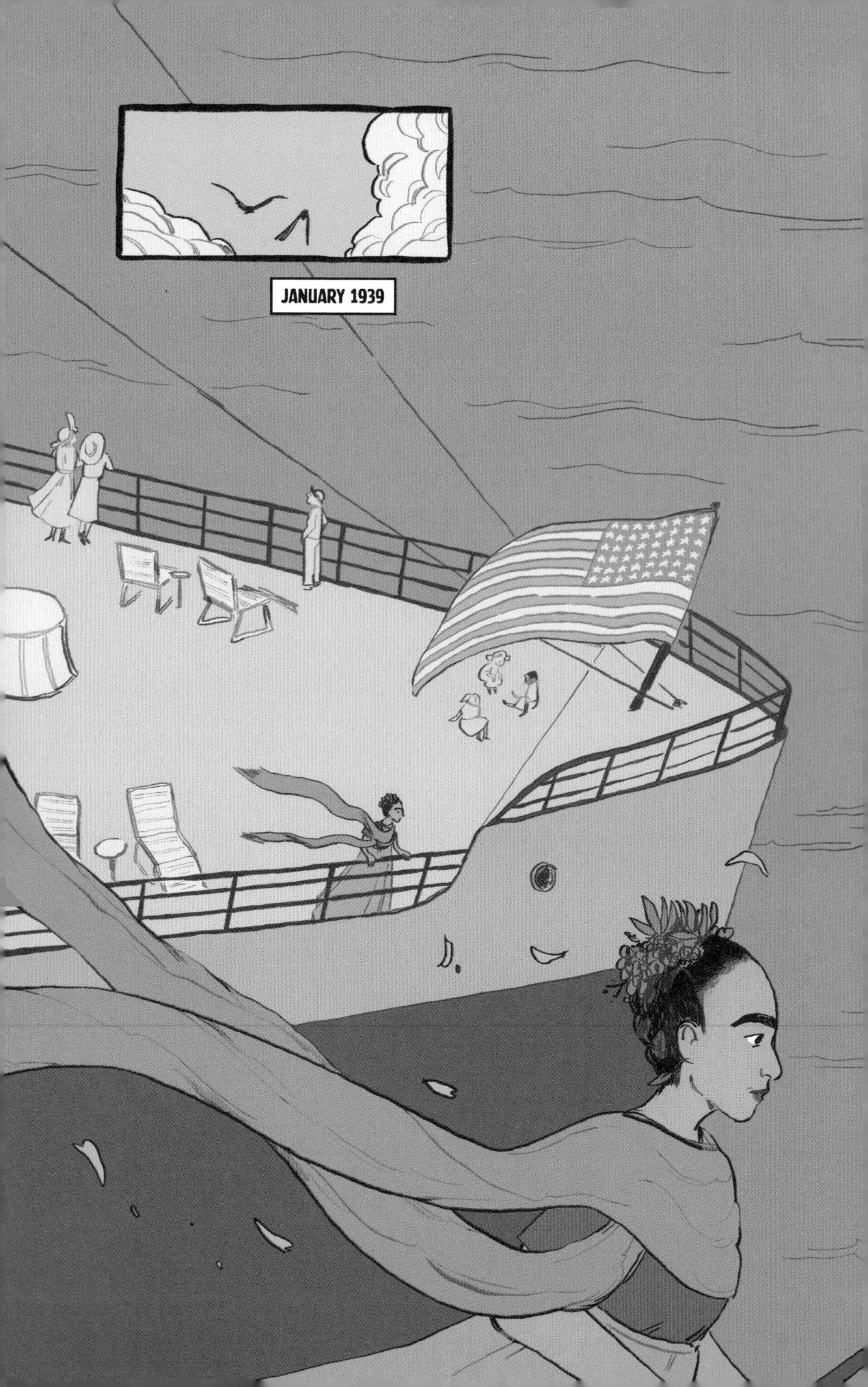
JANUARY 1939

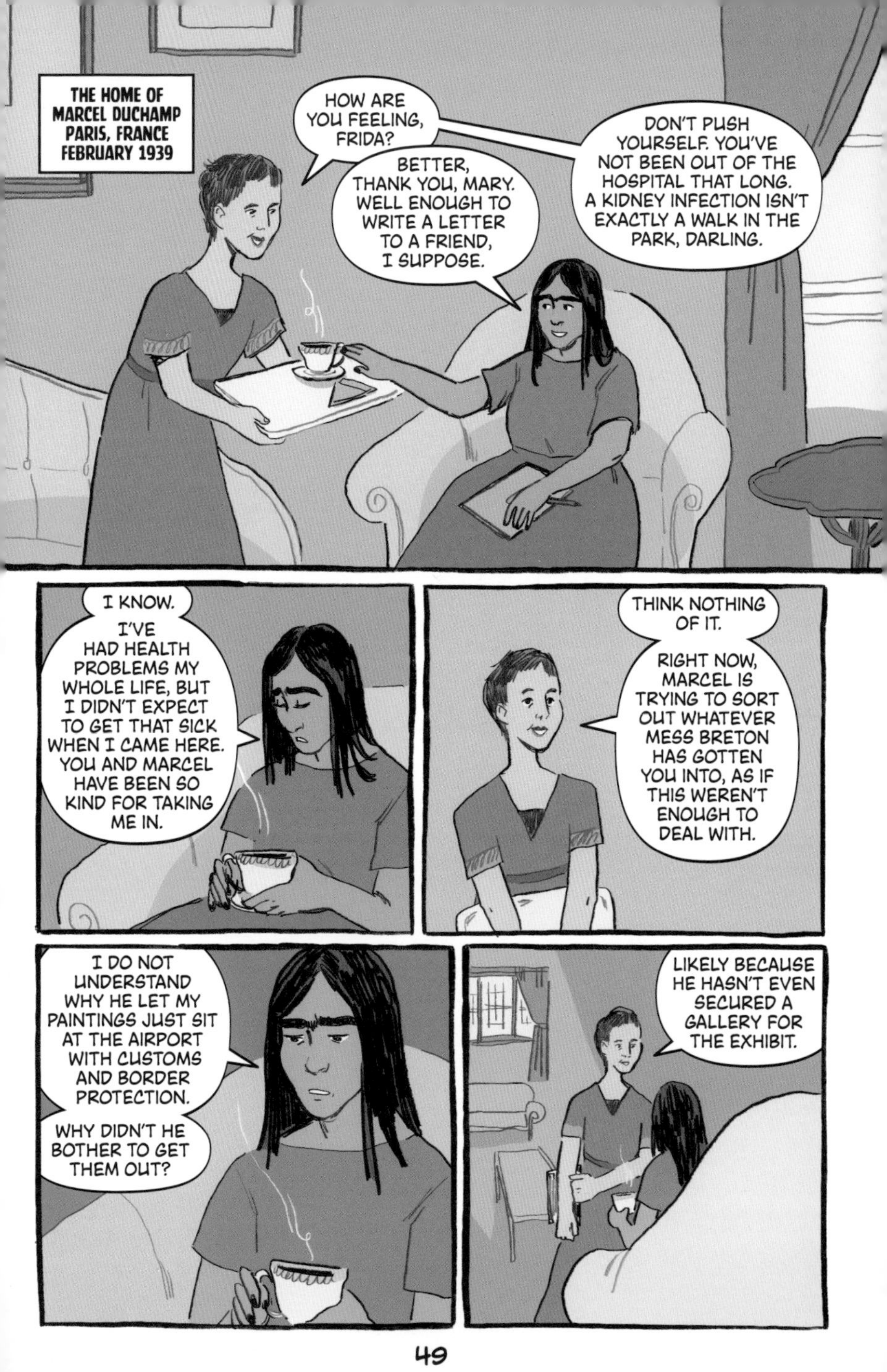
THE HOME OF MARCEL DUCHAMP PARIS, FRANCE FEBRUARY 1939
HOW ARE YOU FEELING, FRIDA?
DON'T PUSH YOURSELF. YOU'VE NOT BEEN OUT OF THE HOSPITAL THAT LONG. A KIDNEY INFECTION ISN'T EXACTLY A WALK IN THE PARK, DARLING.
BETTER, THANK YOU, MARY. WELL ENOUGH TO WRITE A LETTER TO A FRIEND, I SUPPOSE.
I KNOW.
I'VE HAD HEALTH PROBLEMS MY WHOLE LIFE, BUT I DIDN'T EXPECT TO GET THAT SICK WHEN I CAME HERE. YOU AND MARCEL HAVE BEEN SO KIND FOR TAKING ME IN.
THINK NOTHING OF IT.
RIGHT NOW, MARCEL IS TRYING TO SORT OUT WHATEVER MESS BRETON HAS GOTTEN YOU INTO, AS IF THIS WEREN'T ENOUGH TO DEAL WITH.
I DO NOT UNDERSTAND WHY HE LET MY PAINTINGS JUST SIT AT THE AIRPORT WITH CUSTOMS AND BORDER PROTECTION.
WHY DIDN'T HE BOTHER TO GET THEM OUT?
LIKELY BECAUSE HE HASN'T EVEN SECURED A GALLERY FOR THE EXHIBIT.

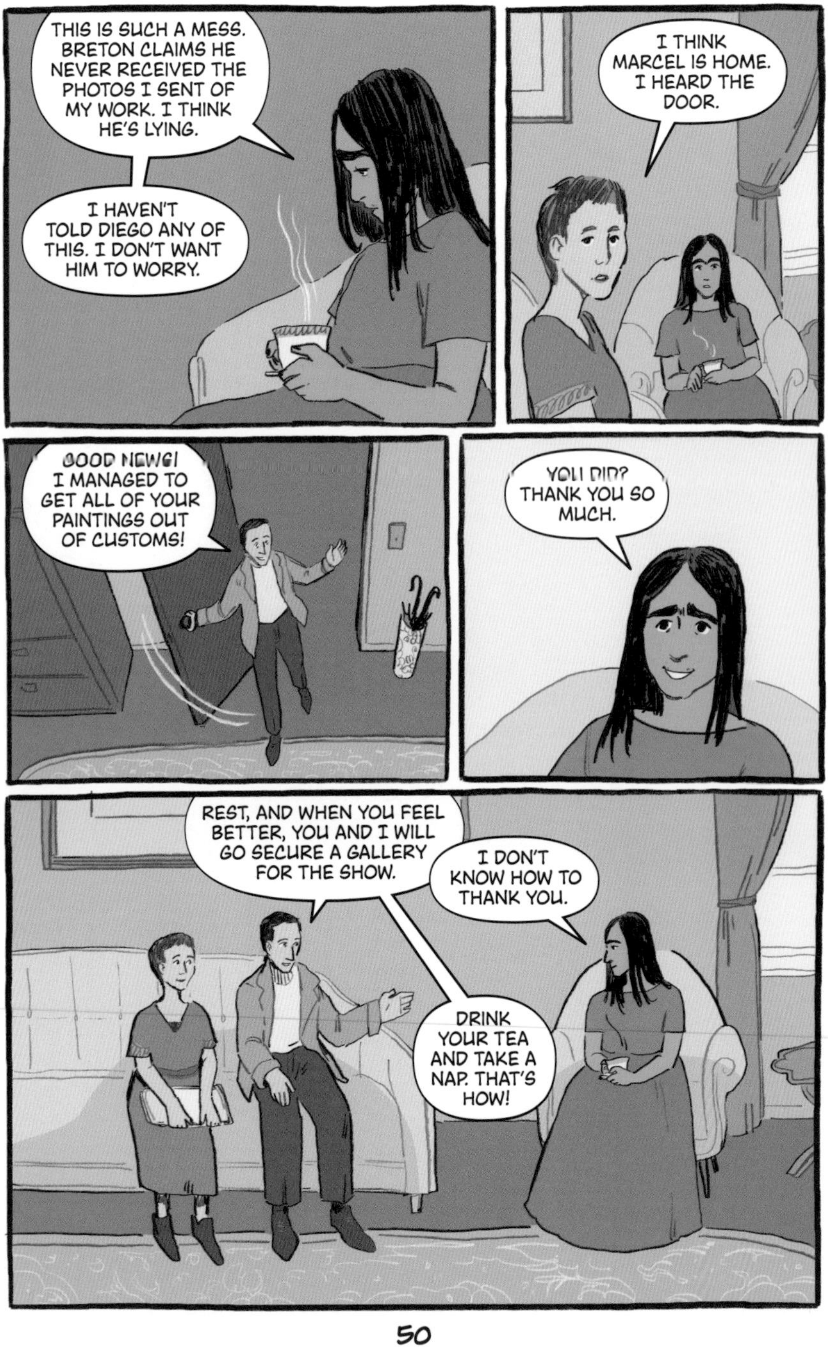
THIS IS SUCH A MESS. BRETON CLAIMS HE NEVER RECEIVED THE PHOTOS I SENT OF MY WORK. I THINK HE'S LYING.
I HAVEN'T TOLD DIEGO ANY OF THIS. I DON'T WANT HIM TO WORRY.
I THINK MARCEL IS HOME. I HEARD THE DOOR.
GOOD NEWS! I MANAGED TO GET ALL OF YOUR PAINTINGS OUT OF CUSTOMS!
YOU DID? THANK YOU SO MUCH.
REST, AND WHEN YOU FEEL BETTER, YOU AND I WILL GO SECURE A GALLERY FOR THE SHOW.
I DON'T KNOW HOW TO THANK YOU.
DRINK YOUR TEA AND TAKE A NAP. THAT'S HOW!

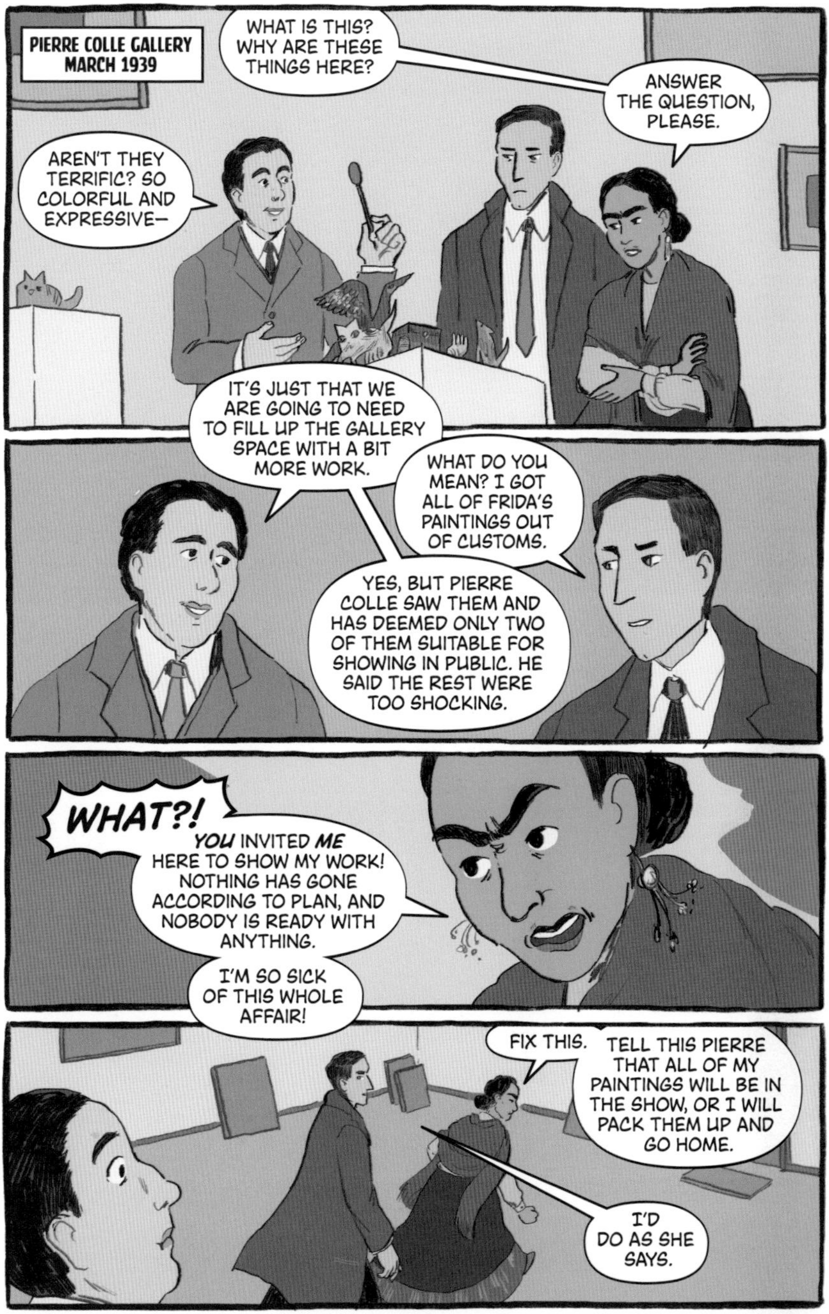
PIERRE COLLE GALLERY MARCH 1939
WHAT IS THIS? WHY ARE THESE THINGS HERE?
ANSWER THE QUESTION, PLEASE.
AREN'T THEY TERRIFIC? SO COLORFUL AND EXPRESSIVE—
IT'S JUST THAT WE ARE GOING TO NEED TO FILL UP THE GALLERY SPACE WITH A BIT MORE WORK.
WHAT DO YOU MEAN? I GOT ALL OF FRIDA'S PAINTINGS OUT OF CUSTOMS.
YES, BUT PIERRE COLLE SAW THEM AND HAS DEEMED ONLY TWO OF THEM SUITABLE FOR SHOWING IN PUBLIC. HE SAID THE REST WERE TOO SHOCKING.
WHAT?!
YOU INVITED ME HERE TO SHOW MY WORK! NOTHING HAS GONE ACCORDING TO PLAN, AND NOBODY IS READY WITH ANYTHING.
I'M SO SICK OF THIS WHOLE AFFAIR!
FIX THIS.
TELL THIS PIERRE THAT ALL OF MY PAINTINGS WILL BE IN THE SHOW, OR I WILL PACK THEM UP AND GO HOME.
I'D DO AS SHE SAYS.

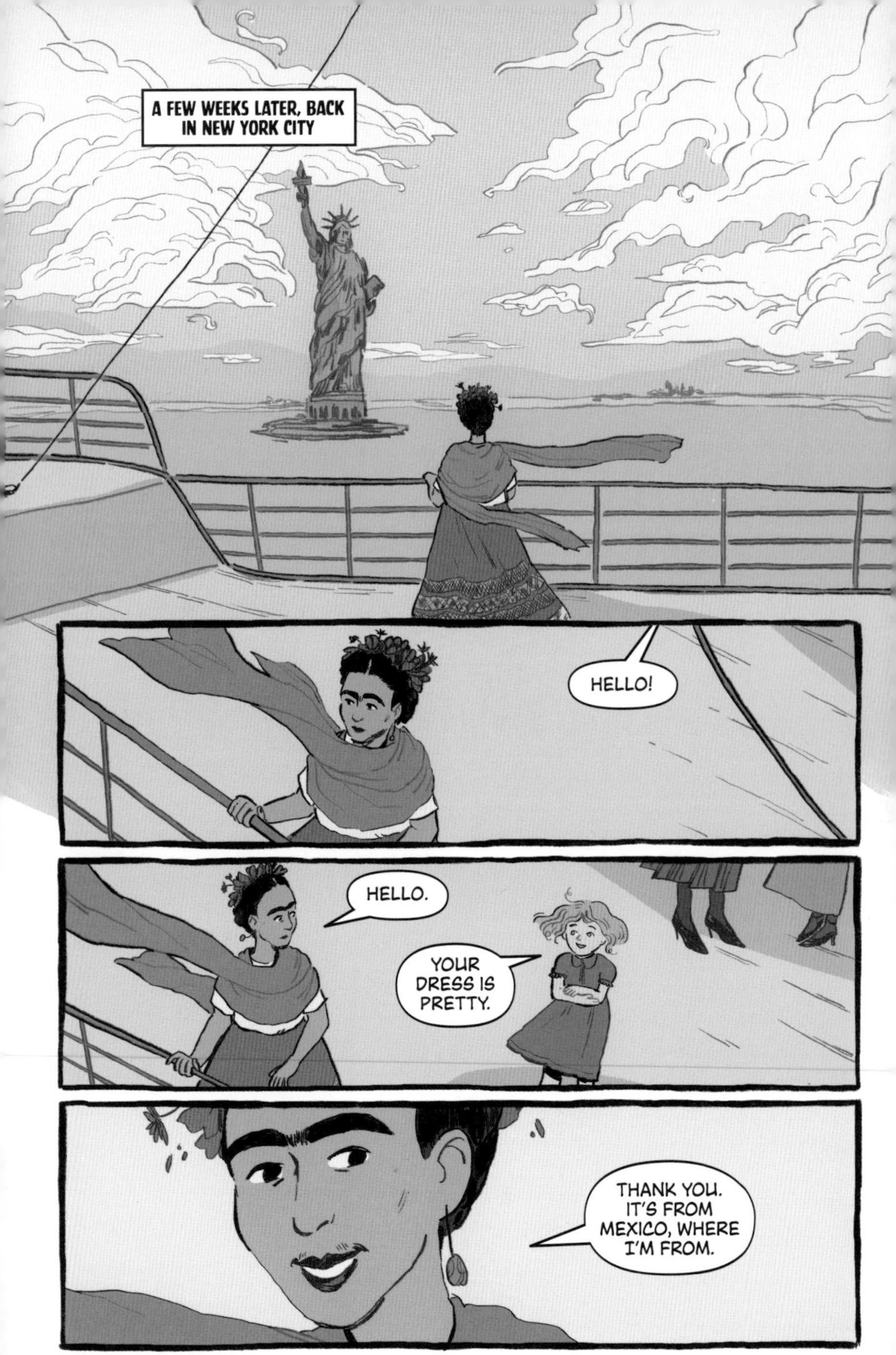
A FEW WEEKS LATER, BACK IN NEW YORK CITY
HELLO!
HELLO.
YOUR DRESS IS PRETTY.
THANK YOU. IT'S FROM MEXICO, WHERE I'M FROM.

Frida's Fashion

A staple of Frida's wardrobe, Tehuana dresses are traditionally worn by women in the isthmus of Tehuantepec in Oaxaca, Mexico. The dresses cover most of the body and consist of a loose-fitting, intricately embroidered cotton blouse called a huipil, a shawl (known as a rebozo), and a long, colorful embroidered skirt. These skirts were often accompanied at the bottom by a white pleated lace ruffle, which was removable and easier to clean. Completing the outfit was the resplendor, a ceremonial lace headdress used for full-dress occasions.

In the years following the end of the Mexican Revolution in 1920, Tehuana fashion began to symbolize Mexican nationalism and ties back to Mexico's indigenous culture. Throughout the 1930s and 1940s, Frida wore this style likely to avoid discomfort when seated with her plaster cast but also to show her Mexican pride. As Frida gained more popularity, the mainstream fashion world took notice of her fashion, too. In 1938, Italian designer Elsa Schiaparelli created "La Robe de Madame Rivera" ("Mrs. Rivera's Dress"), inspired by Frida's Tehuana style. Tehuana style quickly infiltrated the fashion world and has become associated with the idea of female empowerment.

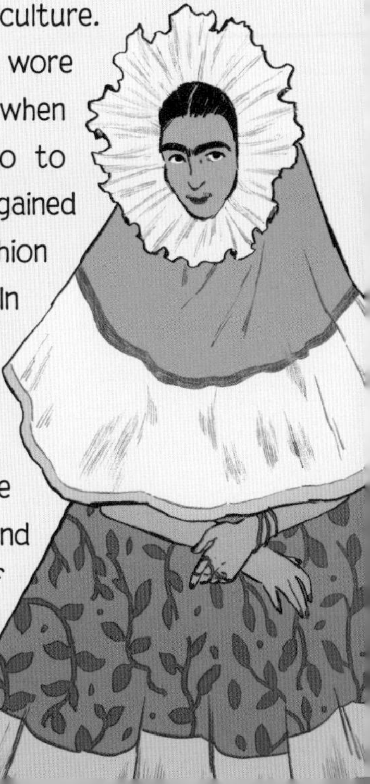

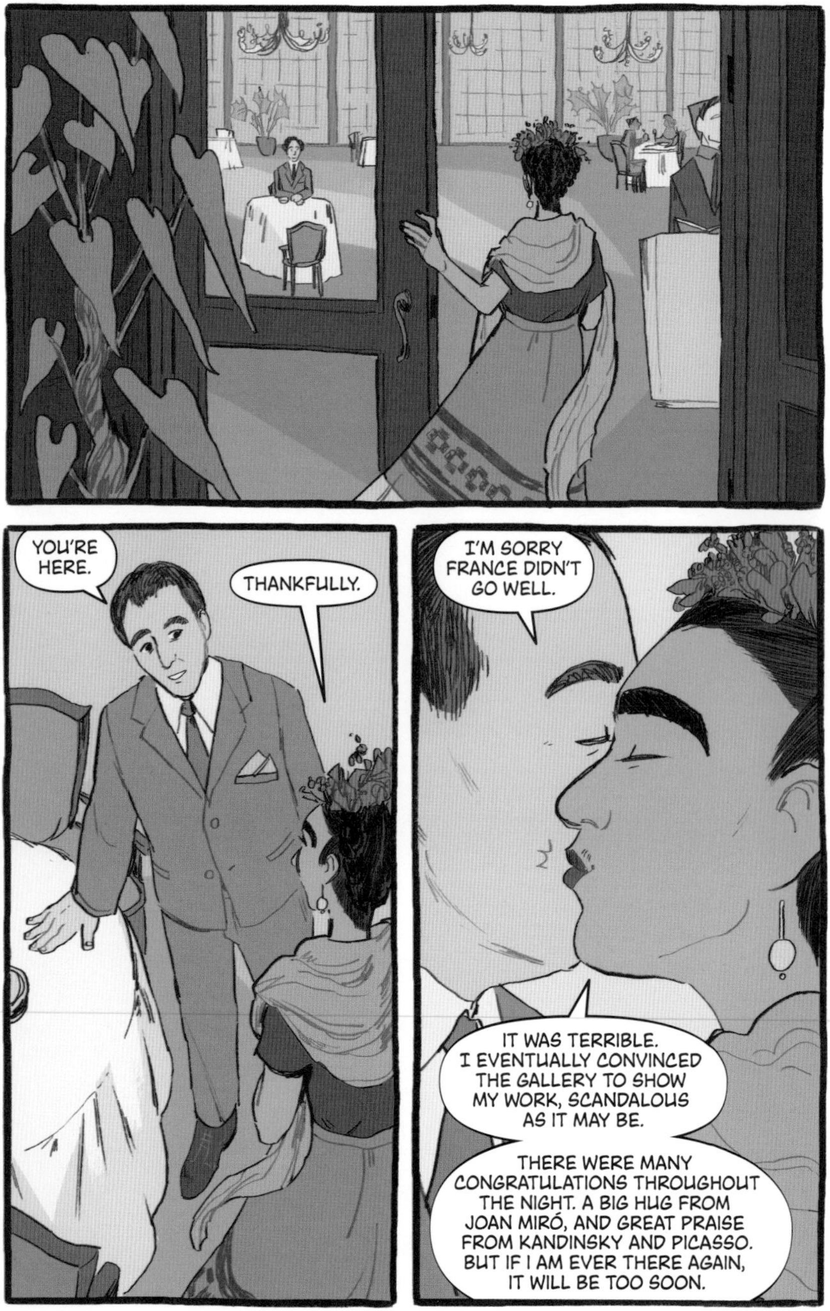
YOU'RE HERE.
THANKFULLY.
I'M SORRY FRANCE DIDN'T GO WELL.
IT WAS TERRIBLE. I EVENTUALLY CONVINCED THE GALLERY TO SHOW MY WORK, SCANDALOUS AS IT MAY BE.
THERE WERE MANY CONGRATULATIONS THROUGHOUT THE NIGHT. A BIG HUG FROM JOAN MIRÓ, AND GREAT PRAISE FROM KANDINSKY AND PICASSO. BUT IF I AM EVER THERE AGAIN, IT WILL BE TOO SOON.

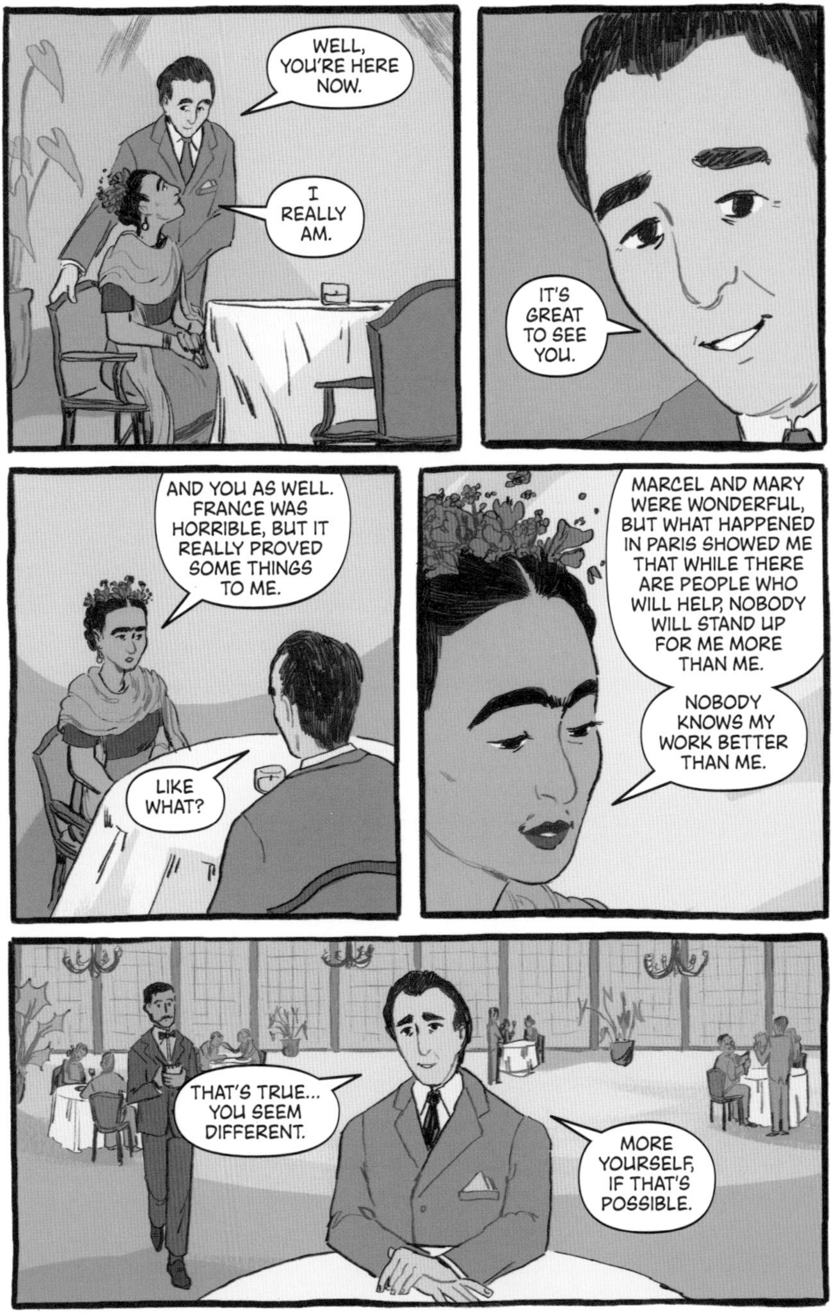
WELL, YOU'RE HERE NOW.
I REALLY AM.
IT'S GREAT TO SEE YOU.
AND YOU AS WELL. FRANCE WAS HORRIBLE, BUT IT REALLY PROVED SOME THINGS TO ME.
LIKE WHAT?
MARCEL AND MARY WERE WONDERFUL, BUT WHAT HAPPENED IN PARIS SHOWED ME THAT WHILE THERE ARE PEOPLE WHO WILL HELP, NOBODY WILL STAND UP FOR ME MORE THAN ME.
NOBODY KNOWS MY WORK BETTER THAN ME.
THAT'S TRUE... YOU SEEM DIFFERENT.
MORE YOURSELF, IF THAT'S POSSIBLE.

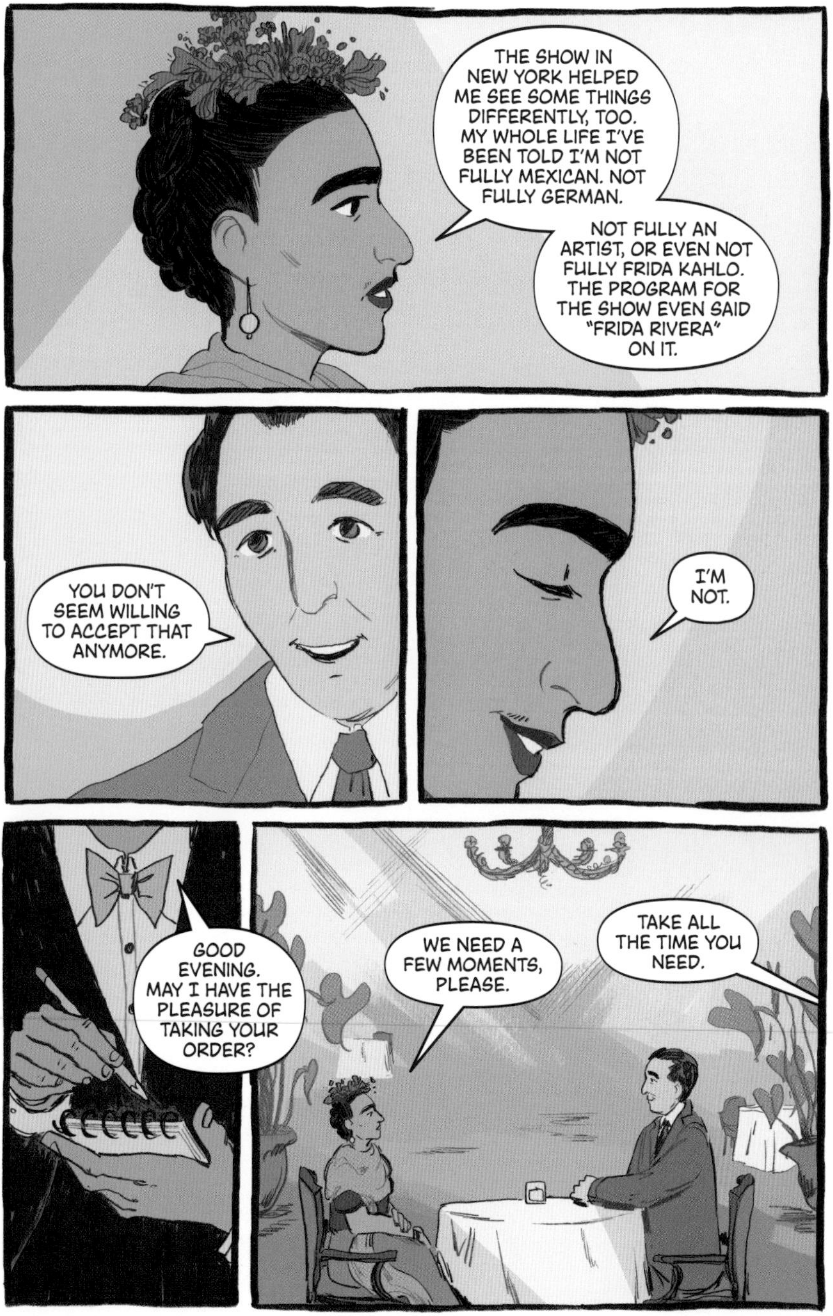
THE SHOW IN NEW YORK HELPED ME SEE SOME THINGS DIFFERENTLY, TOO. MY WHOLE LIFE I'VE BEEN TOLD I'M NOT FULLY MEXICAN. NOT FULLY GERMAN.
NOT FULLY AN ARTIST, OR EVEN NOT FULLY FRIDA KAHLO. THE PROGRAM FOR THE SHOW EVEN SAID "FRIDA RIVERA" ON IT.
YOU DON'T SEEM WILLING TO ACCEPT THAT ANYMORE.
I'M NOT.
GOOD EVENING. MAY I HAVE THE PLEASURE OF TAKING YOUR ORDER?
WE NEED A FEW MOMENTS, PLEASE.
TAKE ALL THE TIME YOU NEED.

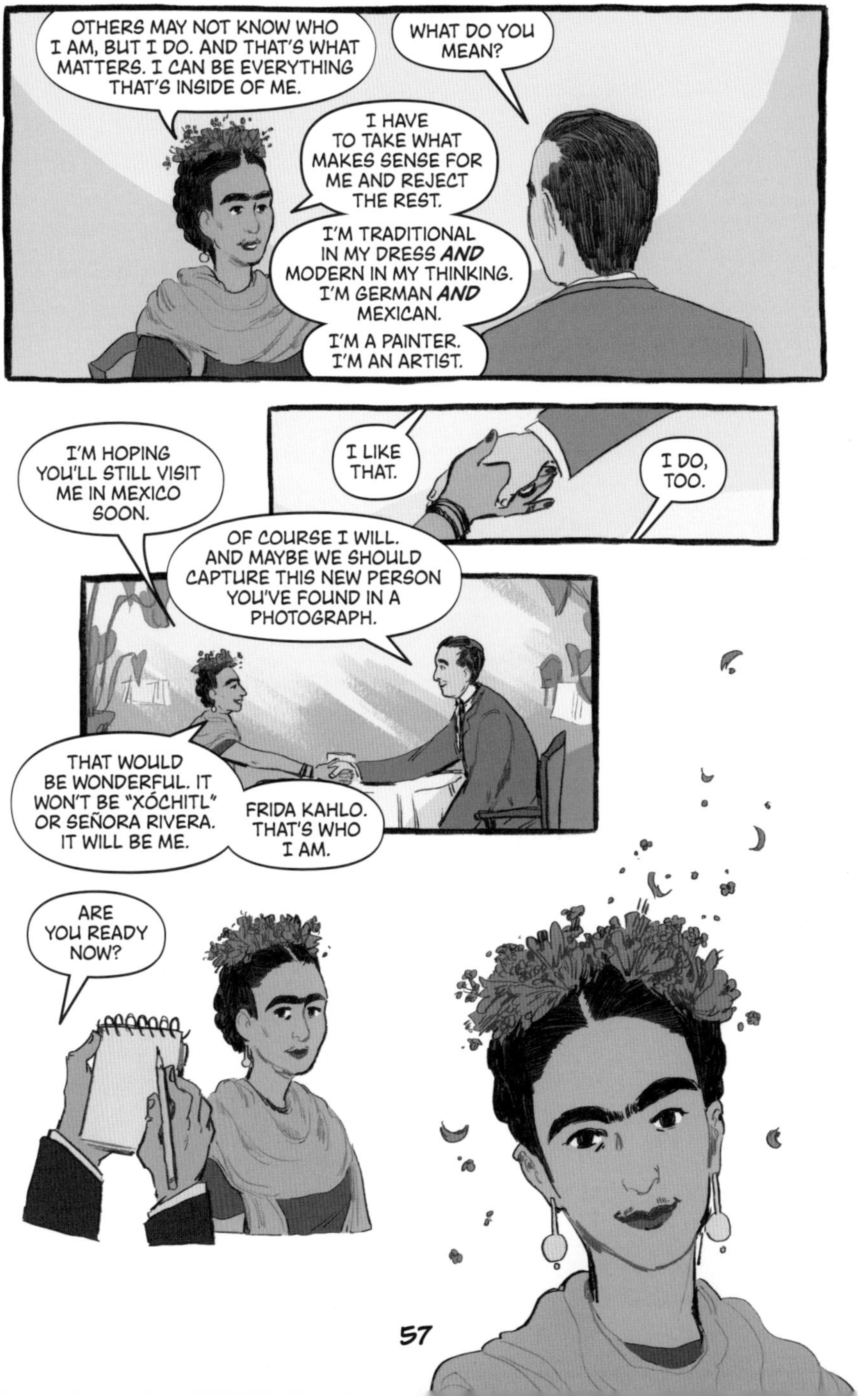
OTHERS MAY NOT KNOW WHO I AM, BUT I DO. AND THAT'S WHAT MATTERS. I CAN BE EVERYTHING THAT'S INSIDE OF ME.
WHAT DO YOU MEAN?
I HAVE TO TAKE WHAT MAKES SENSE FOR ME AND REJECT THE REST.
I'M TRADITIONAL IN MY DRESS *AND* MODERN IN MY THINKING. I'M GERMAN *AND* MEXICAN.
I'M A PAINTER. I'M AN ARTIST.
I LIKE THAT.
I DO, TOO.
I'M HOPING YOU'LL STILL VISIT ME IN MEXICO SOON.
OF COURSE I WILL. AND MAYBE WE SHOULD CAPTURE THIS NEW PERSON YOU'VE FOUND IN A PHOTOGRAPH.
THAT WOULD BE WONDERFUL. IT WON'T BE "XÓCHITL" OR SEÑORA RIVERA. IT WILL BE ME.
FRIDA KAHLO. THAT'S WHO I AM.
ARE YOU READY NOW?

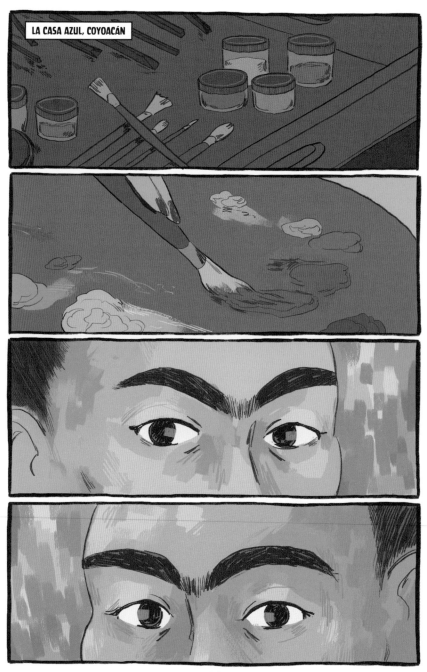

LA CASA AZUL, COYOACÁN

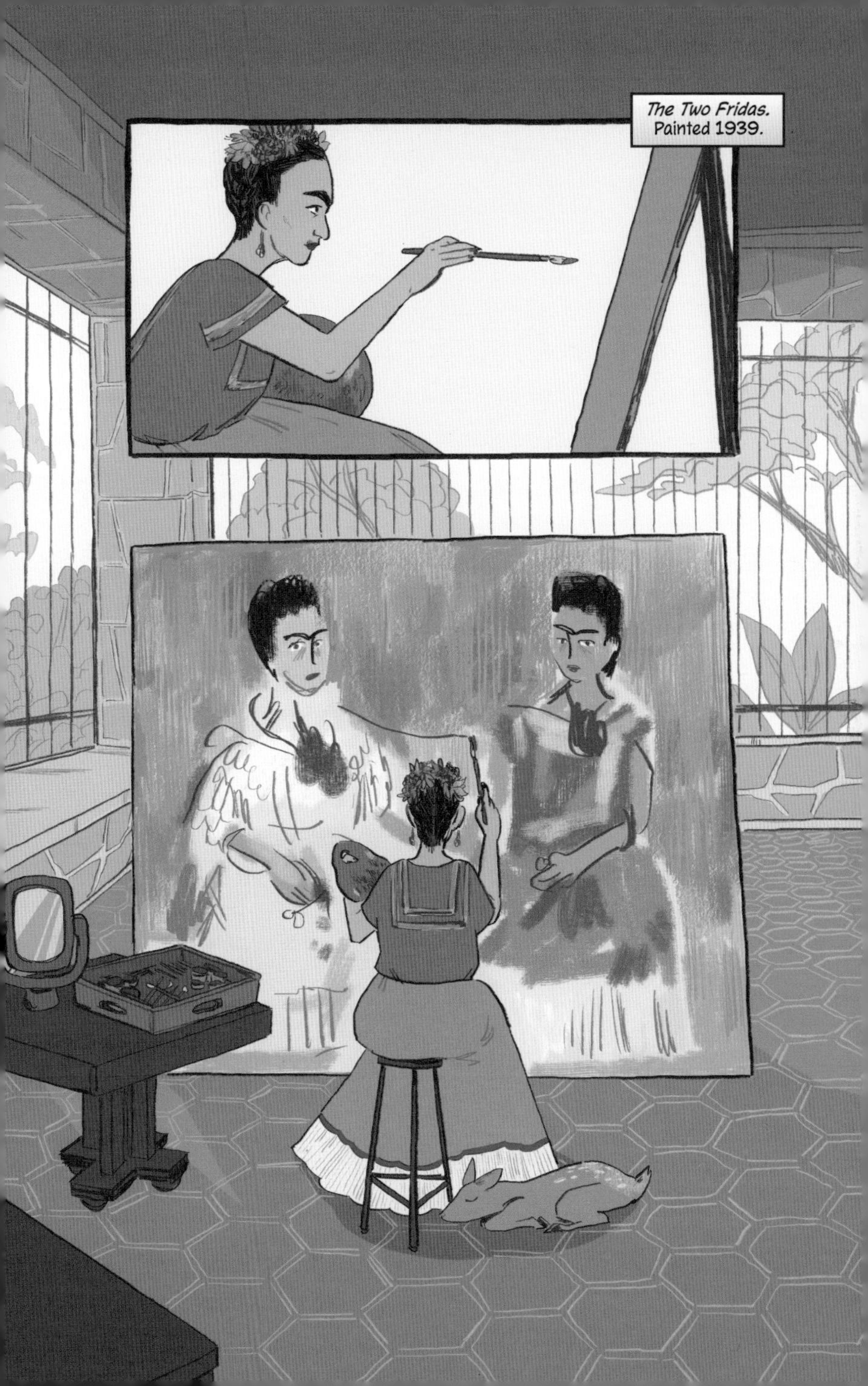
The Two Fridas.
Painted 1939.

Conclusion

After the exhibition in Paris, the Louvre purchased one of Frida's paintings, *The Frame*, which made her the first twentieth-century Mexican artist to be featured there. Both of her shows in New York and Paris launched her career as a respected, mainstream artist.

In the years that followed, Frida's relationship with Diego continued to be rocky. They divorced in 1939 only to remarry a year later. Even while divorced, they remained close, and Frida continued to manage Diego's finances and correspondence. That said, she and Nickolas Muray remained close for the rest of their lives.

During the 1940s, Frida became an art instructor and often taught art students in her home at La Casa Azul and at the Escuela Nacional de Pintura, Escultura y Grabado in Mexico City. She also participated in exhibitions throughout Mexico and the United States.

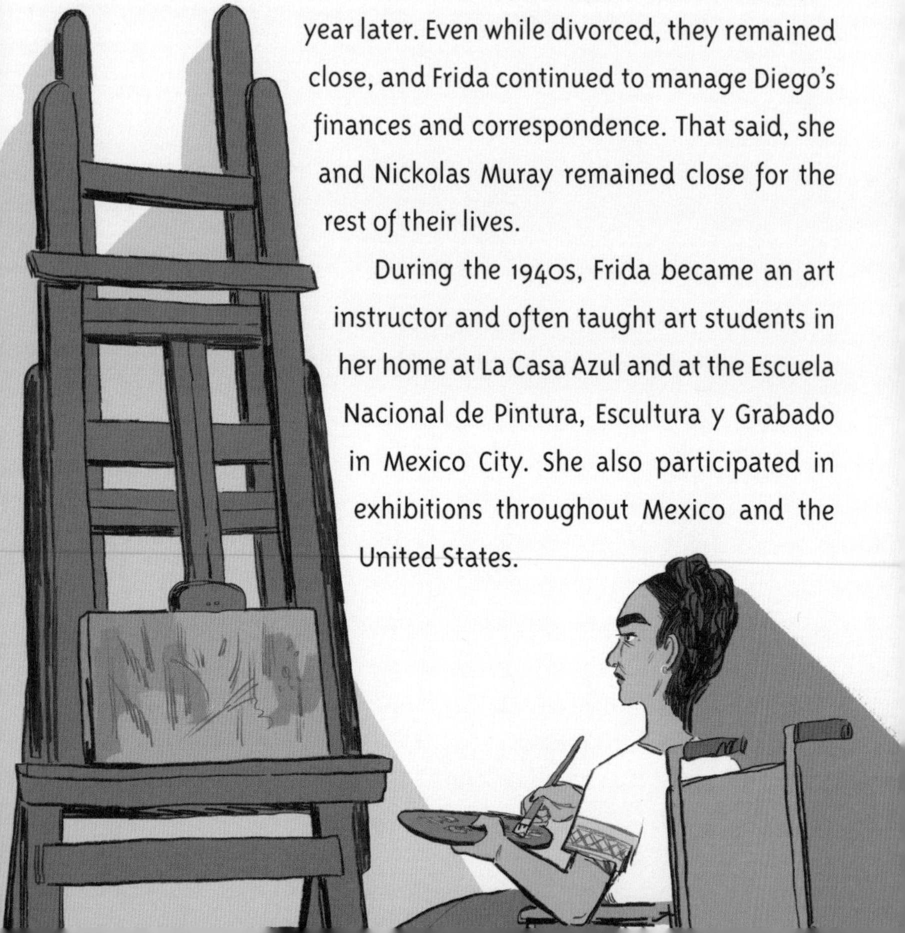

Throughout her forties, her health, which had always been unstable, began to worsen. She had a surgery to strengthen her spine, which unfortunately was not successful. But as her health declined, her art became more well-known and respected. Some of her most famous paintings came from this era, including *The Broken Column* (1944), *Without Hope* (1945), and *The Wounded Deer* (1946). They all vividly showcased how she felt about her declining health and her mortality.

She died in 1954 at the age of forty-seven. She is arguably the most famous Mexican artist, and her home, La Casa Azul, is a museum that showcases her work, her possessions, her clothes, and other personal items. The cultural impact she had on art, fashion, and politics can be seen even today. Her pride in her individuality is what made her body of work personal and honest. She embraced the fact that she was a person of great contradictions, and she took pride in her complicated story. Because of this, the world saw her vulnerability and her talent, which has inspired other artists and people around the world to this day.

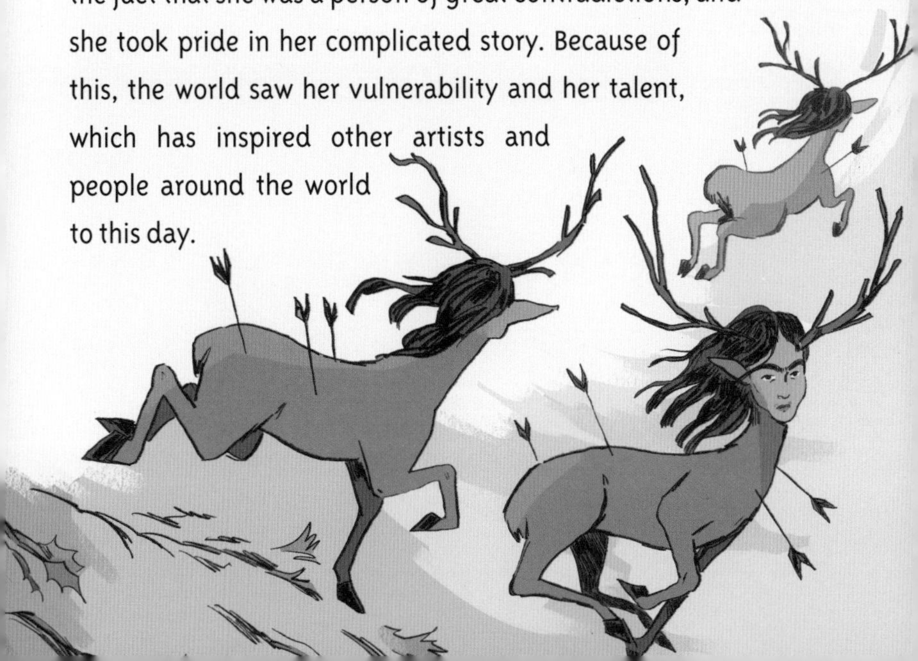

Timeline of Frida Kahlo's Life

1907 — Frida Kahlo is born on July 6

1922 — Meets Diego Rivera when he paints a mural at her school

1925 — Is in a debilitating bus accident on September 17

1929 — Marries Diego Rivera on August 21

1938 — Has her first solo exhibition in New York on November 1

1939 — Has many portraits taken of her by photographer Nickolas Muray

— Participates in "Mexique" exhibition in Paris in March

— Paints *The Two Fridas*

— Divorces Diego in November

1940 — Remarries Diego in December

1953 — Has a solo exhibition in Mexico City in April

1954 — Dies on July 13

1958 — La Casa Azul becomes a museum

Bibliography

*Books for young readers

Alcántara, Isabel, and Sandra Egnolff. *Frida Kahlo and Diego Rivera.* New York: Prestel Publishing, 1999.

Bretaña, Raissa. "Her Own Muse: Fashioning Frida: Opening Night Lecture with Raissa Bretaña." Arkansas Museum of Fine Arts. February 28, 2019. YouTube video, 47:57. https://www.youtube.com/watch?v=Zv_tsGFZfCk&t=1270s.

*Fabiny, Sarah. *Who Was Frida Kahlo?* New York: Penguin Workshop, 2013.

Grimberg, Salomon. *I Will Never Forget You: Frida Kahlo & Nickolas Muray: Unpublished Photographs and Letters.* San Francisco: Chronicle Books, 2006.

Kettenmann, Andrea. *Frida Kahlo, 1907–1954: Pain and Passion.* Köln, Germany: Taschen GmbH, 2003.

Stahr, Celia. *Frida in America: The Creative Awakening of a Great Artist.* New York: St. Martin's Press, 2020.

ABOUT THE CREATORS

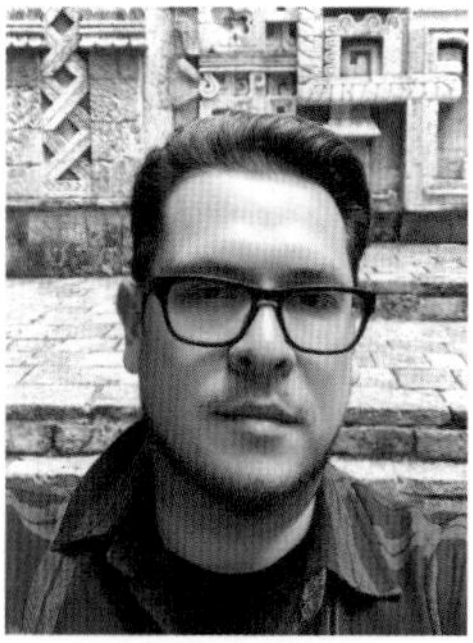

Terry Blas is the illustrator and writer behind the viral webcomics *You Say Latino* and *You Say LatinX* (Vox.com). He has written comics for Ariana Grande and the series *Steven Universe* and *Rick and Morty*. His original graphic novels are *Dead Weight: Murder at Camp Bloom* (Oni Press), *Hotel Dare* (Kaboom!), and *Lifetime Passes* (Abrams/Surely Books, 2021). He is the writer for the Marvel superhero series *Reptil* as well as *Who Was the Voice of the People?: Cesar Chavez* (Penguin Workshop). He lives in Portland, Oregon, with his husband, Scott, and their dog, Alfie.

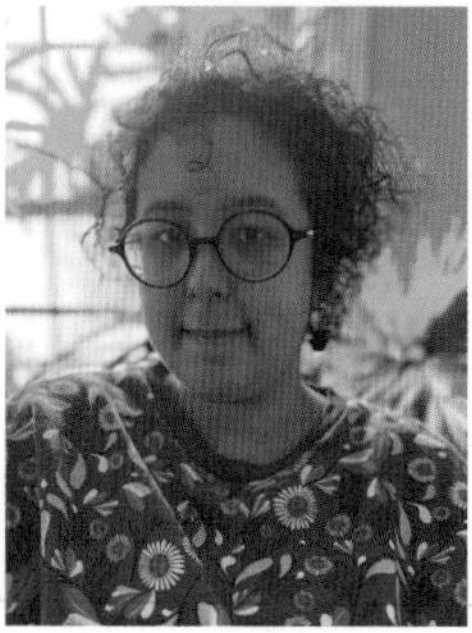

BINGLIN FORTSON-HU

Ashanti Fortson is a cartoonist, illustrator, editor, and educator with a deep interest in difficult emotions, quiet moments, and human connection. Their work explores transience and reflection through a tenderhearted lens. A love for color runs through everything they make. Ashanti's short comic *Leaf Lace* won the 2021 Ignatz Award for Outstanding Comic, and was nominated for Outstanding Artist and Outstanding Online Comic. Ashanti lives in Baltimore with their spouse; their cat, Miss Cheese; and at least three pet rats at all times.